What people are saying about

Western Animism

Mélusine Draco's book takes us back to basics: it explains clearly the fundamentals of Zen and how Zen "Ki" can also be identified with Old Craft "Witch-power". As an old crafter I found the comparison fascinating and also useful. This book has broadened my approach to Craft and has given ideas to try in practice.
Julie Dexter, Dame of Coven of the Scales

I can't think of another writer today who is more unusual or more inspired than Mélusine Draco. I had assumed that, by now, books on Zen were using their one-handed clapping to flog dead horses along roads to nowhere. Yet her take on Zen is completely unexpected and totally original. I don't think she has ever failed to surprise and often startle me in her previous books. This one is no different …
Alan Richardson, esoteric author

Excellent book on Zen, very readable and engaging. Mélusine Draco's father was a martial arts instructor so she grew up with this ancient form of animism-shamanism, and she's well able to relate it across to other traditions. We all come from the same human and spirit roots! This is going to be one of my "go to" books, every time I need a bit of inspiration and to reconnect across the traditions of our Earth.
Elen Sentier, shaman, author and storyteller

Pagan Portals
Western
Animism

Zen & the Art of Positive Paganism

Pagan Portals
Western
Animism

Zen & the Art of Positive Paganism

Mélusine Draco

MOON
BOOKS

Winchester, UK
Washington, USA

First published by Moon Books, 2019
Moon Books is an imprint of John Hunt Publishing Ltd., No. 3 East Street, Alresford
Hampshire SO24 9EE, UK
office@jhpbooks.com
www.johnhuntpublishing.com
www.moon-books.net

For distributor details and how to order please visit the 'Ordering' section on our website.

Text copyright: Mélusine Draco 2018

ISBN: 978 1 78904 123 1
978 1 78904 124 8 (ebook)
Library of Congress Control Number: 2018949287

A CIP catalogue record for this book is available from the British Library.

Design: Stuart Davies

UK: Printed and bound by CPI Group (UK) Ltd, Croydon, CR0 4YY
US: Printed and bound by Thomson-Shore, 7300 West Joy Road, Dexter, MI 48130

We operate a distinctive and ethical publishing philosophy in
all areas of our business, from our global network of authors to
production and worldwide distribution.

Contents

Learn about a pine tree from a pine tree,
and about a bamboo plant from a bamboo.
Basho

For Jan …

Introduction

I Hear Water Dreaming

The term 'pagan' was first used in a derogatory sense by the early Romano-Christian community of southern Europe during late antiquity when referring to unsophisticated country-dwellers; it was later coined as a description of religions other than their own, or the related Abrahamic religions of Judaism and Islam. Today it is generally used to refer to all those who follow a wide variety of traditions (or 'paths') that emphasise reverence for nature and a revival of ancient polytheistic or pantheistic religious practices – in particular within shamanism, Druidry, Norse, Wicca and traditional witchcraft. Japanese Shinto is one of the oldest extant and indigenous animist beliefs in the world that teaches the future comes from the present, as the present is derived from the past.

Animism, of course, is derived from the Latin word *anima* meaning breath or soul. The belief is probably one of man's oldest, with its origin most likely dating to the Palaeolithic age if those wondrous cave paintings are anything to go by, because from its earliest beginnings it is obvious it was a belief that a soul or spirit existed in every object, even if it was inanimate. Was that why the tribal shaman retreated into the darkness of the caves, perhaps with some notion of drawing power out of the cave walls themselves? The term 'animism' was first popularised by Sir Edward Burnett in his work *Primitive Culture* (1871) and dismissed as being just that – primitive belief. While none of the world's monotheist religions are animistic (though they may introduce modern animistic elements to cultivate the support of the environmentalists), most other religions – e.g., those of tribal/pagan peoples – are.

By contrast, Zen is the Japanese variant of *Chán*, a school of

Mahayana Buddhism which uses meditation to give an insight into one's true nature – a total state of focus that incorporates a complete togetherness of body and mind. Zen is a way of being: it also is a state of mind. Zen meditation is not only concentration, but also awareness: being aware of the continuing changes in our consciousness, of all our sensations and our automatic reactions. Zen, of course, is not of Japanese origin. In the mid-sixth century it was brought to Japan from China via Korea but the line between Buddhism and Shinto can be decidedly hazy. And despite the impact of this imported belief and philosophy, Japan's interpretation has always remained distinct from its neighbours in its application.

The country's deep-rooted tendency to adapt and transform what it borrows from other cultures manifested itself, and many Buddhist sects that took root or emerged in Japan soon became, and have remained, uniquely Japanese. Zen offered an intellectualising philosophy that also transformed and heightened the indigenous folk-beliefs. When Zen practice is combined with the ancient faith of Shinto, it becomes a non-religious but highly spiritual path of enlightenment that is completely at home in the twenty-first-century Western mindset.

Shinto has always represented the lure of the outdoor spaces – the sand, the wind, the stars, the waves, the hum of the insects, the music of the waterfall, while Shintoists believe that the same wonderful forces that move in Nature move in themselves. There is no difference because there is no dividing line between divine and human. For this reason an individual's belief and their lifestyle have entered into each other so that it is almost impossible to tell where one begins and the other ends. To the thoughtful this is as it should be. Why should belief be something 'added onto' a person's life?

Nevertheless, judging from the amount of postings on the Internet, an increasing number of pagans appear to be taking more heed of negative thoughts than they do positive ones; and to have a good balance in our life, we need to have at least three positive thoughts to each negative one every day. And, according to Dr Maureen Gaffney's self-help book, *Flourishing*, in order to flourish and thrive, the ratio of positive to negative needs to be at least six to one! Positive thoughts are all about the little things in life, and being aware and grateful for them – just as we are advised to do in the opening lines of William Blake's poem, 'Auguries of Innocence':

> *To see a World in a Grain of Sand*
> *And a Heaven in a Wild Flower*
> *Hold Infinity in the palm of your hand*
> *And Eternity in an hour ...*

Or William Henry Davies's 'Leisure' that most of us can still quote from our schooldays:

> *What is this life if, full of care,*
> *We have no time to stand and stare.*
> *No time to stand beneath the boughs*
> *And stare as long as sheep or cows.*
> *No time to see, when woods we pass,*
> *Where squirrels hide their nuts in grass.*
> *No time to see, in broad daylight,*
> *Streams full of stars, like skies at night*

Being positive about life is not about winning the Health Lottery or harbouring the ambition of having your home featured in *Spirit & Destiny* magazine – it's more about taking time to appreciate white clouds against the bright blue of a winter sky; the whisper of falling rain; the aroma of freshly baked bread; the perfume of sweet peas fresh from the garden; or the texture of stone and the colours of a butterfly's wings – the list is endless. What's more, if we make a practice of seeking out the positive, we tend to find it everywhere – even on really 'bad, black dog' days when we can still hear water dreaming, or listen to the stones growing.

MD

Chapter One

A Singularly Zen Idea

Man's space on earth ...
A quick Hunt or shelter
Before the rain comes down.
Sogi

Looking back I can see how my Shinto upbringing (my father was a martial arts instructor and a countryman) made it so easy to pick up on the underlying animistic threads of Old Craft and its associated esoteric practices. From a small child I was in touch with that indefinable sensation of witch-power, god-power, *ki, qi,* or earth energy – call it what you will – the natural energy that is believed to be an active principle forming part of any animate or inanimate thing. Similar concepts can be found in many cultures: *prana* in Hinduism (and elsewhere in Indian culture); *chi* in Chinese; *pneuma* in ancient Greece; *mana* in Hawaiian culture; *lüng* in Tibetan Buddhism; *manitou* in the culture of the indigenous peoples of the Americas; *ruah* in Jewish culture, and 'vital energy' in Western philosophy.

Ki, I soon learned, was the unseen life force in our body and everywhere. It was the universal energy that penetrates everywhere uniting all manifestations of the universe, visible or invisible, animate or inanimate. For example, the ancient Masters noticed that animals' reaction times were much faster than man's. They also had more endurance and were fiercer fighters; they could be quieter or louder. This observation led to the belief that this was because the animals were more at one with themselves since their *ki* flowed undivided and remained focused.

The Masters came to the conclusion that animals possessed

5

this unique ability because they weren't burdened with something that we humans have: consciousness. This meant that in animals nothing intervenes between stimuli and response, idea and action, mind and body. Their breathing pattern was different to that of a human. Animals faced with danger composed themselves by taking a deep breath – then lashed out as they exhaled sharply. Many animal moves intrigued the ancient Masters and some eventually became the basis for various martial art styles. This was the first understanding of the *practical* advantages of this unseen life force.

In *Traditional Witchcraft and the Path to the Mysteries* and because there is no official pagan litany, I used a lot of Shinto belief and Zen philosophy to demonstrate how the elevation of the mind leads to higher understanding regardless of the Path being followed. For the traditional Japanese there is no dividing line between the divine and human, since the forces that move in Nature move in man, according to Zen teaching:

When one looks at it, one cannot see it:
When one listens for it, one cannot hear it:
However when one uses it, it is inexhaustible.

Even the rocks are possessed of the divine spark and often form part of the intricate designs used to create those beautiful Zen gardens for contemplation – reflecting the belief that the 'Buddha-nature' is immanent not only in man, but in everything that exists. I used this quote in one of the first esoteric books I had published – *What You Call Time* – and I find that I have come full circle in trying to explain that everything, magical and mystical, really just comes down to this basic understanding (and acceptance) of *ki* – or whatever you like to call it!

From me flows what you call time ... comes from the music of Japanese composer, Toru Takemitsu, who seems to 'hear unimaginable ideas in his head and translates them into sound through the most extraordinary means' – and who, in turn, took the title from a poem by the Japanese poet Makoto Ooka: 'Clear Blue Water'. The orchestral piece is in part inspired by the Tibetan idea of the wind horse, an allegorical conception of the human soul, familiar to many in the well-known associated sequence of five coloured flags, representative of the elements: fire (red), water (blue), earth (yellow), sky (white) and wind (green).

Unfortunately, within contemporary paganism, there appears to be a widening schism between those who are immediately at one with these thoughts – and those who need to assume the *outward* trappings of esoteric practices to enhance their personalities and elevate their standing in the eyes of others, without bothering to develop the inner Self. There was an amusing instance just recently when a close colleague was told by a 'celebrity witch', that I couldn't possibly have the antecedents I claim, because there was nothing written about them in my books! *'Well, there wouldn't be, would there?'* came the response. I don't happen to feel the need to add every jot and tittle to my writing in order to convince the readership that I have indeed walked the Path of the Mysteries.

Those who study with me are the ones who reap the benefit of this received wisdom – not those who would only gain their knowledge from reading a wide assortment of esoteric books. In Zen it is the question that is most important – not the answer. And there is also understanding the concept of 'secret teaching' that always seems to rattles the cages of certain people in the magical community because they never stop to think of it as merely referring to the kind of teaching that cannot be set down in words but can only be learned through experience.

These differences are also reflected in an increasing violence of speech within social media directed at those who do not share the same opinion over what are generally considered to be pagan issues. I might even go so far as to say, that I find the level of personal intolerance far greater than it was when I first entered the pagan community back in the day. Columnist John Masterson summed it all up recently when he wrote: 'We live in an era where legions of people are dying to take offence, often on behalf of others ... and the result is bland society and boring [people] politics. ... Yes, there are a lot of whingers around who find it difficult to find any good anywhere, anytime and "talk radio" would immediately die without a constant stream of whiners, whingers and offended people but I could live with that,' he concluded. Social media, too, would take a hammering but judging from the growth of mediocre postings that dominate of late, I suspect, too, that many objective, sensible, and intelligent pagans have just folded their altar cloths and quietly stolen away.

As an antidote, may I suggest that in the spirit of Zen it is possibly necessary to step away from this type of negative thinking and try seeing the world through the 'way of the *kami*'. Folk Shinto (as opposed to State Shinto) includes numerous folk beliefs in supernatural agencies and spirits, and the practice of divination, ancestor worship, and shamanic healing. Some of these practices have been imported from Buddhism, Taoism and Confucianism, but the majority come from ancient local indigenous traditions that literally do trace their origins back to their hunter-gatherer ancestors. There are also many locations of stone ritual structures, refined burial practices and early *tori* that strengthened the continuity of primal Shinto; and at some point there was a recognition that the ancestors created the current generations and so the deep reverence of the Ancestors (*tama*) took shape. Here we find plenty of parallels between Eastern and Western paganism.

And I am not the only Western 'pagan' to recognise this juxtaposition. As Jon Moore wrote in *Zen Druid: A Paganism for the 21st Century*, earth-based spirituality is the bedrock of human interaction with Nature, the Cosmos and our fellow human beings. 'In times of great change while the impetus is for reassessment and renewal, the field has become confused with different schools and methodologies. There are arguably now as many schools as there are practitioners.'

For all its ancient roots, however, Shinto remains the largest religion in Japan, practised by nearly eighty per cent of the population, yet only a small percentage of these identify themselves as 'Shintoists' in national surveys unless they belong to an established sect. Most Japanese attend Shinto shrines and pray to *kami* without belonging to any formalised religion, since there are no formal rituals required to become a follower of folk Shinto. According to Inoue Nobutaka [*Shinto, a Short History*], this is because Shinto even has different meanings in Japan. 'In modern scholarship, the term is often used with reference to kami-worship and related theologies, rituals and practices. In these contexts, "Shinto" takes on the meaning of "Japan's traditional religion", as opposed to foreign religions such as Christianity, Buddhism, Islam and so forth.' And according to the Shinto section of *The World's Great Religions*:

The Japanese find comfort and inspiration in the beauties of their surroundings. They have built their shrines in spots of breath-taking beauty. They try to keep themselves constantly attuned to the loveliness all about them:

E'en in a single leaf of a tree
Or a tender blade of grass,
The awe-inspiring Deity
Manifests itself.

The practice of beauty leads the Japanese to participate in ceremonies and festivals that may seem strange to us. The Insect-Hearing Festival is an example of this. On a quiet evening in the early weeks of autumn, they sit quietly and listen to the noises of various insects. Just as typical is the story of the Zen teacher who stepped before his class one day to give a lecture.

He paused to listen to the song of a bird outside the window, and then he dismissed the class. There are sermons in nature – and the Japanese hear them freely.

This is surely paganism at its most pure and one we can easily identify within the West without having to embrace the religious doctrines of the East because this old agrarian and animistic-based belief focuses on the existence and power of the *kami* that exist in nature, and throughout Japan – and the rest of the world. *Kami* or *shin* is often defined in English as 'god', 'spirit', 'spiritual essence' – all these terms merely meaning 'the energy generating a thing'. Though the word *kami* is translated multiple ways into English, no one English word expresses its full meaning. 'The ambiguity of the meaning of *kami* is necessary, as it conveys the ambiguous nature of *kami* themselves' (Historical Dictionary of Shinto).

And since the Japanese language does not distinguish between singular and plural, *kami* refers to the divinity, or sacred essence, that manifests in multiple forms. Rocks, trees, rivers, animals, places, and even people can be said to possess the nature of *kami*. *Kami* and people exist within the same world and share its interrelated complexity. *Kami* refers particularly to the power of phenomena that inspires a sense of wonder and awe (the sacred) in the beholder, testifying to the divinity of such a phenomenon. And if we strip away all of the Western labels and jargon concerning what is and what isn't paganism, surely this becomes the most all-encompassing description of all: *kami*.

In Shinto there is a much more casual approach to interacting with *kami,* since they certainly are the most ambiguous of 'spirits' and although they require deep reverence and respect, they are not personifications of deity like the Horned God, or the many goddesses that have crept into the contemporary pagan pantheon. As Sokyo Ono explains in Shinto, the Kami Way: *kami* are not separate from nature, but are of nature, possessing both positive and negative, and good and evil characteristics. They are manifestations of musubi, the interconnecting energy of the universe.

> The kami reside in all things, but certain objects and places are designated for the interface of people and kami. There are natural places considered to have an unusually sacred spirit about them, and are objects of worship [veneration]. They are often mountains, trees, unusual rocks, rivers, waterfalls, and other natural things. In most cases they are on sacred ground or near a shrine. The shrine is a building in which the kami is housed. It is a sacred space, creating a separation from the mundane world. The kamidana is a household shrine that acts as a substitute for a large shrine on a daily basis. In each case the object of worship is considered a sacred space inside which the kami spirit actually dwells, being treated with the utmost respect.

Interestingly, this is a faith about an overall perspective more than a simple list of beliefs. This perspective – referred to by the phrase mono no aware – is a uniquely Japanese way of seeing the world and its beauty that contains many nuances, which include:

Aesthetic sensitivity – a sense of beauty and of the beautiful;

Sensitivity toward the aesthetic and the emotional as a basis for looking at life – this includes the sadness or pathos of life as well as joy, happiness and bliss;

Seeing with the heart into the natural beauty and goodness of all things.

These sensibilities underpin much of what is focused upon in Shinto/Zen thought and artistic expression – things such as nature, harmony, balance – and their particular expression in practical and decorative arts such as flower arranging, architecture, landscape design, the tea ceremony and much else. These are outward expressions of our inner harmony (*wa*) that encourages us to spend evenings gazing at the moon; or sitting for hours contemplating the beauty of a garden, or a flower arrangement, or even a drop of rain on a single twig or leaf.

Many of today's disenfranchised pagans in the West, however, appear to be seeking a spiritual connection to life without feeling the need to become a witch, a Wiccan, a shaman, Heathen, or a Druid. Here the Shinto approach fulfils the basic need for a belief system based on what we would define as simple animism and ancestor worship in accordance with the world's other authentic, animistic traditions such as the Australian Aboriginal and Native American way of life; while Zen provides the intellectual stimulation rising from the simplicity of basic folk-belief to elevate the soul to a higher level of mysticism. As Jon Moore also observed in *Zen Druid*:

> It represents and creates the possibility for growth and development in all areas, from the common everyday to the mystical. The mystical is then embodied in – and becomes – the everyday; in other words, from ignorance of how the world works to enlightenment. It is a journey to the very centre of the individual and out to the edges of the cosmos, for in the knowing of ourselves is the knowing of the universe.

What should also appeal to those of a non-religious but spiritual bent is the fact that Shinto beliefs are not dogmatically centred around any official creed or codified system of theology, or ethics – instead there is a distinct sensibility that underlies an entire approach to life and the world. This can be captured not only with that phrase *mono no aware*, but also with the concepts of *makoto* ('sincerity in the heart') and *kannagara-no-michi* (that virtue is inseparable from the rest of life, especially life lived in harmony with the natural world).

Examined more closely, much of the 'philosophy' surrounding Shinto and Zen would sit comfortably against that which passes for modern paganism and/or spirituality in the Western world with its platitudes and questionable antecedents. Or the multi-million pound businesses that cater for the need of magical regalia in terms of books, crystals and divinatory equipment! What finer act of worship could there be in any language or culture than to simply hold a fragile blossom of a wild flower in the palm of the hand in order to connect with the divine without the need to consult the tarot cards.

A student of Zen should learn how to read
the love letters sent by the snow,
the wind and the rain.

The Kensho Moment (East)

If you have read so far and found yourself thinking: 'This is what I've always wanted but have never been able to put into words or feelings', then that is a kensho moment. This is a Japanese term from the Zen tradition. *Ken* means 'seeing', and *shō* means 'nature' or 'essence'. It appears suddenly and fleetingly, upon an interaction with something or someone else; on hearing, seeing or reading some significant phrase, or by experiencing an unexpected sight or sound. *Kenshō* is an initial insight or awakening. And we might experience numerous 'kensho moments' along the way – in the Western traditions we refer to them as 'portals' or 'gateways' – and we must pass through several on the path to Understanding and/or Enlightenment (*satori*).

In authentic Zen teaching this experience would be followed by further intense training to deepen this insight, so that the student learns to express it in daily life; but for the purpose of this text we will be looking at 'spontaneous kensho' – which can happen without any formal application. Dennis Genpo Merzel, an American Zen and spirituality teacher relates what he describes as an 'awakening experience' following a breakup of a serious relationship when he was in his late twenties.

> I was feeling very confined and conflicted. I needed to get some space, so I went out to the Mojave Desert for a three-day camping weekend with two friends. On the Friday, I hiked up a mountain alone. I knew nothing about meditation or spiritual practice. I was just sitting there, thinking about my life and the things going on. I felt I had gotten pretty screwed up for such a young age. I could see my VW camper, my home for the weekend, parked a few miles away. But at the same time, I was aware that my home was back in Long Beach, California. And a natural koan came to me: Where is home? All of a sudden, I had a kind of breakthrough. I felt myself fall away, and I became one with the cosmos, one with the universe, one with all things. I knew in that moment that wherever I am, that is home; home is everywhere. I also knew who I was, beyond description, but let's call it Big Mind. That experience completely changed my life.

In truth this was no big deal and we've all been there. Sitting on a rock or under a tree, feeling emotionally or mentally drained when a sudden thought comes to us and there is an immediate uplifting of the spirit. We may or may not immediately recognise it as such, but if we attempt to hold on to that moment, odds-on we may come up with a solution to our problem. On the other hand we may, of course, choose to ignore the sensation and dismiss it as something inconsequential – and continue to wallow in our misery.

The experience may not be a spiritual moment in the accepted sense of the word but it is there if we know how to see it. For example, today is a sunny, blustery late autumn morning and the rooks are out in full force. They are engaging in a display of what is known as 'tumbling' and the noise is deafening; the westerly wind is bringing in squalls and showers off the ocean, bringing the warm thermals that carry the birds high up into the air. Then they drop, tumbling and twisting in flight as they plunge earthwards and the wind carries them further up the Glen along with the falling leaves. A little while later they return and the performance is repeated. The experts don't know why they indulge in this mad autumnal behaviour but since these are among some of the most intelligent animals on the planet, perhaps they do it purely for fun; as some kind of community bonding in a spirit of joie de vivre that is infectious. Watch these antics against the backdrop of a clear blue sky and it is a happiness that transcends species.

This is also a kensho moment since it is unexpected and uncontrived but the happiness of the birds communicates itself to the watching human and for brief moment that joy is shared. It is an emotion that crosses the divide when the antics of a wild animal stimulates laughter in the heart of a human – especially if it is recognised and accepted as a rare, uplifting encounter.

A Magical Truth (West)

This is a term used in Western paganism to describe a profound piece of received information, wisdom or philosophy that is pertinent to all spiritual paths and traditions, regardless of origin or ethnic background. These 'truths' are usually discovered in non-magical books of both fiction and non-fiction. As Allen Bennett observed it's that moment in reading when you come across something ... 'a thought, a feeling, a way of looking at things – which you thought special and particular to you. Now here it is, set down by someone else, a person you have never met, someone even who is long dead. And it is as if a hand has come out and taken yours.'

The writer probably hasn't the remotest connection to religion or mysticism but suddenly there is this illumination, this insight – an idea that triggers your own train of thought along spiritual (or mystical) highways and byways you'd never thought to travel. That's why I love Chet Raymo's books because they are full of magical truths from the pen of a most unlikely source: a Catholic school-educated Professor of Physics and Astronomy who can write about everyday happenings as though they provide the most magical insights on Earth – which, of course, is exactly what they do! Or as St Bernard of Clairvaux pointed out: 'More things are learned in the woods than from books; trees and rocks will teach you things not to be heard elsewhere.'

Like all countries across the globe, Japan has some spectacular scenery and its people have a great love of the natural world, but Japan also happens to be one of the most crowded places on the planet, so there is a great community spirit attached to the celebrations. There is an abundance of local festivals – *matsuri* – connected with shrines throughout the country and most are held annually. These are mostly agrarian-based festivals to celebrate the changing of the seasons, special historical events, or connected with fertility, and prayers to the 'gods' for good health – bearing in mind that although Japan is in the southern hemisphere the emphasis on the agrarian calendar nevertheless gels with Western (northern hemisphere) pagan traditions.

Most festivals in Japan are colourful, lively and joyous affairs often involving a procession with participants in period dress or *happi* coats carrying through the streets a *mikoshi* – a special, decorated palanquin containing the local Shinto *kami*. Many festivals also involve large, decorated floats, exhibitions of martial arts such as archery and horse-riding, music, dancing and copious quantities of food and drink served up from *yatai*, or street stalls. None of this, of course, has any real connection to religion per se but has all the trappings of a local village fete or County Show where people can connect with their roots and the community spirit.

Needless to say, Japan has its own cosmogony, mythology and folk-heroes that play an important part in its interpretation of the arts – just as a considerable amount of Western art and literature focuses on Arthurian legend. Izanagi is the forefather of the gods and the first male as well as the god of creation and life. He and his wife, Izanami, were responsible for the birth of the islands of Japan and many *kami*, though she died in childbirth; later, after his failed attempt to retrieve her from the underworld, he sired Amaterasu, Susanoo and Tsukuyomi.

Izanami is Izanagi's wife and sister, and the first female as well as the goddess of creation and death. She died shortly after the birth of Kagu-tsuchi, and Izanagi followed her to the underworld, but failed to bring her back to the living world. A marital spat between the pair caused the cycle of life and death for all living beings.

Kagu-tsuchi's birth burned his mother Izanami, causing her death. His father Izanagi, in his grief, beheaded Kagu-tsuchi with his sword, Ame no Ohabari, cutting his body into eight pieces, which became eight volcanoes. The blood that dripped off Izanagi's sword created a number of deities, including the sea god Watatsumi and rain god Kuraokami. Kagu-tsuchi's birth, in Japanese mythology, comes at the end of the creation of the world and marks the beginning of death. In the Engishiki, a source which contains the myth, Izanami, in her death throes, bears the water god Mizuhame, instructing her to pacify Kagu-tsuchi if he should become violent. This story also contains references to traditional fire-fighting tools: gourds for carrying water and wet clay and water reeds for smothering fires that often appear in traditional literature.

Amaterasu is the goddess of the sun as well as the purported ancestress of the Imperial Household of Japan; for many reasons, one among them being her ties to the Imperial family, she is often considered (though not officially) to be the 'primary god' of Shinto. Tsukuyomi-no-Mikoto is the god of the moon. He killed the goddess of food, Uke Mochi, out of disgust and anger in the way she had prepared a meal. This caused Amaterasu to never face him again, causing the sun and moon to be in different parts of the sky.

Susanoo-no-Mikoto is the god of storms as well as in some cases the god of the sea. He is also somewhat of a trickster god, as Japanese mythology extensively documents the 'sibling rivalry' between him and Amaterasu. Susanoo also was responsible for the slaying of the monster Yamata no Orochi and the subsequent discovery of the sacred sword Kusanagi – one of the Three Sacred Treasures of Japan. The regalia represents the three primary virtues: valor (Kusanagi – the sword), wisdom (Yata no Kagami – the mirror), and benevolence (Yasakani no Magatama – the jewel).

According to legend, these treasures were brought to earth by Ninigi-no-Mikoto, legendary ancestor of the Japanese imperial line, when his grandmother, the sun goddess Amaterasu, sent him to pacify Japan. These treasures were eventually said to be passed down to Emperor Jimmu, who was the first Emperor of Japan and was also Ninigi's great-grandson. Traditionally, they are a symbol of the emperor's divinity as a descendant of Amaterasu, confirming his legitimacy as paramount ruler of Japan. When Amaterasu hid in a cave from her brother Susanoo-no-Mikoto, thus plunging the world in darkness, the goddess Ame-no-Uzume-no-Mikoto hung the mirror and jewels outside the cave and lured her out of the cave, at which point she saw her own reflection and was startled enough that the gods could pull her out of the cave. Susanoo later presented the sword Kusanagi to Amaterasu as a token of apology.

There are, of course, numerous other deities who appeared frequently in the traditional arts, some of the more familiar being Fūjin (also known as Kami-no-Kaze), he is the god of the wind and one of the eldest Shinto gods, said to have been present at the creation of the world. He is often depicted as an *oni* with a bag slung over his back; Hachiman, the god of war and the divine protector of Japan and its people. Originally an agricultural deity, he later became the guardian of the Minamoto clan whose symbolic animal and messenger is (ironically to Western thinking) the dove; and Inari Ōkami, the god or goddess of rice and fertility whose messenger and symbolic animal is the fox.

On the plum blossoms
Thick fell the snow;
I wished to gather some
To show thee,
But it melted in my hands.

The Kensho Moment: Exercise

And last, but certainly not least, we should never lose sight of the Path of the Hearth Fire and all its attendant superstitions, which often gets abandoned in the search for more loftier cosmic wisdom. The Hearth Fire is Love in *all* its various aspects; the source of womanly power and manly energy in its most sacred but most simplistic forms, and without it no other fire can come into existence. The Greeks (Hestia) and Romans (Vesta) had their goddesses of the Hearth and every home had its family altar on with offerings were made to the *lares familiaries*, the spirits who were particularly venerated at the domestic hearth on appropriate calendar days and on occasions of family importance. The welcoming Hearth Fire is the symbol of domesticity and peace – and is the most precious focus of all.

Similarly, nearly every Japanese home has a *kamidana* or household shrine, traditionally placed on a shelf high on the wall and dedicated to the ancestors and household *kami*. But unless we are genuinely observing authentic Shinto rites it would be more appropriate to install a *tokonoma*, a built-in recessed alcove in which items for artistic appreciation are displayed. *Tokonoma* first appeared in the late Muromachi period and is basically a wall space where a scroll is hung, with a low raised dais in front for setting out a vase for flowers. The items usually displayed in a *tokonoma* are calligraphic or pictorial scrolls and flowers. *Bonsai* and *okimono* (ornamental figurines) are also sometimes displayed there, although traditionally, *bonsai* were considered to be too dirty for such a highly respected place!

A *tokonoma* is the perfect focus for meditation or relaxation and if we can set this up in a quiet corner of the home where we can light a candle and/or incense burner, it becomes our own oasis of calm in a busy world. The scroll can be replaced by any picture(s) that we find soothing or uplifting, and the items we choose to decorate the alcove should be simple and uncluttered – unlike a traditional pagan altar that often resembles a church jumble sale than a focus for prayer or meditation! Flower arrangements can be large seasonal blooms in a substantial container, or a delicate arrangement of two or three stems in a tall, narrow bud vase.

The setting up of this alcove (or small table if space is at a premium) is a humble act of creating a non-devotional space where we simply can be. It is there to help focus the mind and combat the stress of modern living. Household accessories are removed when not in use so that the *tokonoma* found in almost every Japanese house, is the focal point of the interior.

Snow-capped as they are,
The gentle slopes of the mountains
Fade into the hazy mist
At twilight on a spring day.
Basho

Chapter Two

A Zen Approach to the World, the Universe and Everything

For these few days
The hills are bright with cherry blossom.
Longer, and we should not prize them so.
Yamare no Akahito

The most famous of all Japanese rituals must be the *hanami*, or 'flower viewing', the traditional custom of enjoying the transient beauty of flowers and almost always referring to those of the cherry (*sakura*) or, less frequently, plum (*ume*) trees. From around the first of February on the island of Okinawa and the end of March to early May, cherry trees bloom all over the islands. The blossom forecast – cherry blossom front – is announced each year by the weather bureau, and is watched carefully by those planning *hanami* as the blossoms only last a week or two. In modern-day Japan, *hanami* mostly consists of having an outdoor party beneath the trees during daytime or at night. *Hanami* at night is called *yozakura* or 'night *sakura*' and in many places temporary paper lanterns are hung in the trees for evening enjoyment.

An even more ancient form of *hanami* also exists in Japan, which is enjoying the plum blossoms, which is referred to as *umemi*, or 'plum-viewing'. This kind of *hanami* is popular among older people, because events are calmer than the *sakura* parties, which usually involve younger people and can sometimes be very crowded and noisy. The proverb 'dumplings rather than flowers' hints at the real priorities for most cherry blossom viewers, meaning that people are more interested in the food and drinks accompanying a *hanami* party than actually viewing the flowers themselves!

The custom was originally limited to the elite of the Imperial Court, but soon spread to samurai society and, by the Edo period, to the common people as well. Traditionally, poems would be written praising the delicate flowers, which were seen as a metaphor for life itself, luminous and beautiful yet fleeting and ephemeral. This was said to be the origin of *hanami* in Japan.

Nevertheless, every country in the world has a seasonal 'moment' when national vegetation bursts into flower. Here in the British Isles we can take the time to appreciate the stark contrast of snowdrops in a winter wood; the azure carpet of bluebells in early summer; or the banks of brilliant rhododendrons in a local arboretum. Or on a more traditionally pagan level, view the clouds of delicate blackthorn flowers against the bare, black branches; followed by the foamy cream blossom of the hawthorn with its remarkable perfume. Take the ubiquitous flask and sandwiches of the intrepid British picnicker, find a quiet log – preferably by a stream – and create your own *hanami* moment by simply viewing the flowers of your own homeland.

Broadly speaking, Shinto focuses on matters relating to this world, on procreation and the promotion of fertility (both in its widest and literal sense), on spiritual purity and physical well-being; Zen on the other hand, is more concerned with detachment from real life and places greater emphasis on the search for the unknowable. Unexpectedly enough, this latter appealed greatly to the samurai class, and in Zen there is a tradition of composing a poem at the moment of death, which often gives powerful expression to that sense of detachment that infuses Buddhist teaching. There is the story of the retainer who, when forced to commit *seppuku* out of loyalty to his feudal lord, wrote of death as a sharp-edged sword that cut through the void, and compared it to a cool wind blowing in a raging fire. According to C. Scott Littleton, writing on 'Death and the Afterlife' in Shinto in *Eastern Religions*,

In Shinto belief, the *tama* ('soul') of the deceased continues to exert an influence on the living before it finally merges with the *kami* ancestors from the family of which it is part. The Shinto conception of the afterlife thus reflects the Japanese emphasis on continuity over the generations and the collective identity of family and clan ... Buddhist ideas have for the most part superseded Shinto concepts of regions of the dead – but not entirely. After thirty-three years, the *tama* is believed to lose its individual nature and to merge with the collective body of the family *kami*. These ancestral spirits are said to dwell on a sacred mountain in the heartland of Japan. The amorphous family *kami* are also invoked in ritual, but at a more abstract level than the *tama* of a family member who has recently passed away.

This concept also fits comfortably with the beliefs held within certain traditional elements of British witchcraft and shamanism, wherein this powerful ancestral energy represents our culture, traditions, heritage, lineage and antecedents. These 'ancestors' trace the long march of history that our predecessors have taken and when those of a particular Tradition pass beyond the veil. Their spiritual essence merges with the divine spirit of the Whole, which in turn gives traditional witchcraft and shamanism the continuing power to endure – even past its own time and place in history – and in many instances may already have endured for hundreds of years.

Interaction with these spirit-ancestors as an invisible and powerful presence is a constant feature of traditional British Old Craft, for example, with the Ancestors remaining important members of the Tradition or people they have left behind. Reverence is part of the ethic of respect for those who have preceded us in life, and their continued presence on the periphery of our consciousness means that they are always with us. And because traditional witchcraft is essentially a *practical* thing, the Ancestors are called upon to help find solutions to problems through divination, path-working and spell-casting.

Having said this, purity rituals are common across Shinto practice, which points to the need for purity in one's own heart. This purity of heart is a natural companion to *makoto* 'sincerity of heart' and what my old Craft tutor, Bob Clay-Egerton, called 'sincerity of intent'. Purity rituals use water as the cleansing agent, and the customary Shinto rituals include rinsing the mouth, washing the hands, bathing, standing under waterfalls, and other such things. Often, these activities are done at a shrine, and they symbolize the inner purity necessary for a truly human and spiritual life. That is the purpose of the familiar water-basin (*tsukubai*) so that guests may purify themselves before entering a shrine.

Japan has one of the largest populations in the world but nearly three-quarters of the country is uninhabited simply because the forests are too dense and the mountain slopes so steep that the interior in almost impenetrable. Plus, it is also situated on a geological fault with ten per cent of the world's active volcanoes bubbling away beneath the surface and causing some fifteen-hundred earthquakes every year, which means that Nature is at the forefront of everyone's mind.

Nevertheless, this is not 'nature-worship' as we think of it in the West, which is summed up by *Britannica* as, 'Nature as an entity in itself, in contrast with human society and culture or even with God, is a philosophical or poetic conception that has been developed among advanced civilizations.' It covers any religion that worships the earth, nature, or fertility gods and goddesses, such as the various forms of goddess worship or matriarchal religion. Or the 'Gaia philosophy' (named after Gaia, Greek goddess of the Earth), a broadly inclusive term for related concepts that living organisms on a planet will affect the nature of their environment in order to make the environment more suitable for life.

For the Japanese, the world around us is inhabited by *kami* and endlessly animated by the divine. Shinto focuses on Nature itself with simple rituals that propitiate both good and bad *kami* in order to foster good relationships between the human world and the *kami* world. When they pray to these 'spirits of gods', it is not demonstrating any great faith, it is showing great *respect* because the idea of religion is not based on the faith, but based on respect for those all-inclusive customs, traditions and ancestral beliefs of the past, present and future.

In Zen, the relationship between humans and Nature is also particularly important and teaches that we should value *everything* around us. Zen doesn't rely on scriptures or dogma but instead tries to encourage an intuitive understanding of the world through meditation and repeated *practical* exercises. And while meditation is very important, Zen also places great emphasis on practical tasks such as gardening, cooking, flower arranging and the creative arts. Because if we are merely reading about such things we are only acquiring knowledge but by putting them into practice we are enhancing our understanding. So, through rigorous application of practical exercises, we can often find insight from within ourselves. And this is the key characteristic of Zen practice.

And in what appears to be in direct contrast, the influence of Shinto and Zen allowed the violent existence of the samurai to be tempered by wisdom and serenity. As journalist and student of Zen, Barbara Hoetsu O'Brien explains, the first school of Buddhism in Japan was Rinzai, and late in the thirteenth century, samurai began to practise Zen 'because the intensive concentration of Rinzai-style meditation can be an aid in enhancing martial arts skills and reducing fear of death on a battlefield'.

However, it appears the majority of Zen-practicing samurai sought the mental discipline to be better warriors but were not so keen on the Buddhism part of Zen. Yes, Zen influenced the samurai, as it did most of Japanese culture and society for a time. And yes, there is a connection between Zen and Japanese martial arts. Zen originated in China's Shaolin monastery, so Zen and martial arts have long been associated. There is also a connection between Zen and Japanese flower arranging, calligraphy, poetry (notably *haiku*), bamboo flute playing and the tea ceremony. And while many samurai did practice Zen meditation for a time, most weren't all that religious about it.

The contemplative aspect of Zen meditation, however, is to demonstrate that one mind can never understand everything and enables the mind to wander in any direction it pleases. It pursues the unanswerable, the mysterious, because the answer isn't the point of meditation – it is the searching for understanding while appreciating that it is a search that will never end – and why we should value the unknowable. As Dr James Fox explained in *The Art of Japanese Life*, as he explored the connections between Japanese culture and the natural environment: 'The Zen preference for uncertainty and suggestiveness might seem alien to our fact-loving, empirical, positivistic Western outlook but it is impossible to understand unless we embrace the beauty of mystery.'

In a perfect circle
Rises the spring day,
But it gains an enormous length
By the time it sinks
Basho

The Kensho Moment: Exercise
If we want to include something more reverential in our observations, or within our scared space, nothing can be more

useful than the Japanese greeting of a bow (*o-jigi*) that can range from a small nod of the head to a deep bend at the waist. A deeper, longer bow indicates respect and conversely a small nod with the head is casual and informal. This is probably the feature of Japanese etiquette that is best known outside Japan and is considered extremely important, so much so that children normally begin learning how to bow from a very young age. Generally speaking the longer and deeper the bow, the stronger the emotion and respect being expressed.

At the altar within our sacred space we bow twice, clap our hands twice, and then bow once to pray having made some form of appropriate offering. To conclude, we bow twice and clap our hands twice. This clap has the same meaning as a hand clap to express happiness or appreciation. It expresses our joy of meeting with the deity and respect towards the deity.* (It is also the equivalent of clapping our hands within traditional witchcraft to 'earth' ourselves after a magical working or ritual.) Now with our hands still together, we express our feeling of gratitude in our mind without speaking and make a final bow. ***Traditionally the number of bows and handclaps may differ at some shrines.**

On the other hand, our altar may be a mossy stone by a stream; an old stump of a tree in a woodland glade; a venerable old tree, especially a pine ... since this is a practical way of connecting with Nature in a quiet act of contemplation without drawing attention to ourselves. A small nod of the head is far less obtrusive than hugging a tree in a public place!

And if we do have a favourite old tree, there is a simple exercise that enables us to make a real link with the divine. We squat down with our heels as close to the tree as possible and lean back with our spine pressed against the bark and relax. After a while we will feel a tingling, throbbing sensation similar to that which often comes when the blood circulation is restricted in an arm or leg. Needless to say we are tempted to move and change position – but we don't. The throbbing will become a magnified heartbeat that is our own blood pumping through our veins and it may even become slightly uncomfortable and make our head spin.

But if we persevere, the throbbing slowly turns into a strong drumming sensation that feels like it's the tree's very own heartbeat we are grafted into; it is coming from the trunk and branches and reaching down to the very roots themselves. The pressure on the spine increases and can even become quiet painful if the exercise is prolonged but the longer we can sustain the effort the more chance we have of moving away from the here and now, and reaching out for that kensho moment.

The exercise can be stopped at anytime by moving to release the pressure on the spine, but don't try to stand up immediately as you may experience some dizziness until you've become grounded. It may also take several attempts for this sensation to happen but with repeated attempts you will succeed.

The mountain well is frozen hard –
Hard as the ribbon's knot on blue-dyed robes.
How can I hope the ice will melt;
Or that this knot will ever come undone?
Sanekata

Chapter Three

An Alternative Paganism

Regardless of weather,
The moon shines the same;
It is the drifting clouds
That make it seem different
On different nights
Basho

For the seeker of a spiritual mindset without the need for religious belief, the practical simplicities of this approach to animism make it very appealing to the Western perceptions with its twenty-first-century scepticism. Despite being around for millennia, Shinto has no founder, no scriptures and for a long time didn't even have a name. The reverence shown by the Japanese toward Nature, however, stems from Shinto's most ancient and fundamental belief that *kami* govern the natural world and inhabit every aspect of it – the rocks, trees, pools, waterfalls, the flora and fauna, and even natural phenomenon all have their own *kami* – or spirit energy. The world is inhabited by *kami*.

The sky, the flowers, the trees and the beautiful landscape speak to the Shintoist and Zen practitioner of beauty and purity. And so the animist in us looks upon such sights with reverence because we feel the awe in the presence of the pure loveliness of which we are so deeply aware ... and the sacred essence, that manifests in all those multiple forms. *Kami* and people exist within the same world and share its interrelated complexity. *Kami* refers particularly to that power of phenomena which inspires this sense of wonder and awe [the sacred] in the beholder, testifying to its divinity. Nature is venerated and nothing is too small to be of importance.

And there were always the great festivals dating back to the Heian dynasty towards the end of the tenth century mentioned by Sei Shonagon in her *Pillow Book*: 'the New Year and the Blue Horses in winter; the Hollyhock Festival in spring; the summer festival of the Iris, festivals for the Dead, for Chrysanthemums, for First Fruits, and, in October, the exciting Gosechi Dances ...'

Despite the multitude of cultural, historical, mythological and purely national events, the Shinto calendar is still full of interesting holidays, rituals and festivals – some of which can easily be adapted to Western style celebration and observance without involving any religious commitment. Nevertheless, these practices can still provide a channel through which human beings are able to communicate with the festive spirit (*kami*) realm. The following are a few of the simple cross-cultural family or agrarian festivals that would easily adapt to the West because they often coincide with our celebrations of contemporary paganism and traditional folk-festivals.

Silently sitting by the window.
Leaves fall and flowers bloom.
The seasons come and go.
Could there be a better life?

January

In the New Year each house sets up two pines in front of the gate or doorway, one on each side. This decoration is called *matukazari* ('pine decoration') or *kadomatu* ('gate pine'). In certain places, the decoration is limited to pine-trees only, whereas in others, bamboo and plum are used as well. This custom is several hundreds of years old, but its form has changed little by little during its long history. The reason why the pine-tree plays so important a part in the New Year celebrations is that its leaves are evergreen, and it withstands both heat and cold, remaining fresh and vivid throughout the four seasons, and attains an exceeding great age: thus it has the meaning of 'prosperity unchanging forever', and the pine-tree serves as the symbolic expression of this. From olden times, the pine has been chosen as the flower for January (*Floral Calendar of Japan*).

With the New Year also comes a series of personal and domestic festivals that are performed annually for the benefit of house and home. For example:

1 January *Kakizome*

This is the first calligraphy writing of the year in Japan but it is something we can copy on New Year's Day in the West. Make a wish or charm for what you hope the year will bring. Create a simple poem containing words that echo your wishes. Write it in decorative script and add elaborate decoration as a border around the words. Slowly read your words and wishes. Then burn the paper in a fire-proof vessel and release the charm to the elements. Toast the future in sake or wine.

1–3 January *O-shogatsu* (New Year)

Shinto shrines around Japan hold New Year festivals where visitors come to pray for good fortune and good health for the coming year. Similarly in Buddhist temples, visitors come to mark the changing of the year. If you have your own special outdoor place where you go for a moment of quiet spiritual contemplation, now is a good time to pay a visit.

8 January *Dondo Yaki*

Corresponds with the modern Twelfth Night celebrations when *mochi* (rice cakes) are toasted over fires of burning New Year decorations.

10 January *Toka Ebisu*

This is the first major festival of the year – *Toka* means the tenth day, and Ebisu is the god of good fortune in business and prosperity. Though centred on 10 January, this festival actually lasts for five days from the eighth until the twelfth and during this time thousands of visitors crowd into a shrine to conduct a simple ritual of prayer for ongoing success in their work and business. Ebisu is one of the *Shichifukujin,* the Seven Lucky Gods of Japanese folklore, who are traditionally associated with the New Year and is the only one of these seven whose story is home-grown Japanese. Many people buy branches of lucky bamboo grass, called *Fuku-Zasa* which has been blessed in a special ritual by a shrine maiden. They then buy more lucky charms and talismans, which they attach to the bamboo branch. These charms come in all kinds of designs, but two of the most common are treasure boats for wealth and red sea bream for future success. Why not buy a lucky bamboo 'career' plant for the garden (keep it in a pot as bamboo is very invasive) and add paper charms relating to your business or career as the situation demands.

14 January *Seijin no Hi* (Coming of Age Day)

This is a Japanese holiday held annually on the second Monday of January. It is held in order to congratulate and encourage all those who have reached the age of majority (20 years of age) during the past year, and to recognise they have become adults. Festivities include formal 'coming of age ceremonies', as well as after-parties among family and friends. Although 'coming of age ceremonies have been celebrated in Japan since at least 714AD – when a young prince donned new robes and hairstyle to mark his passage into adulthood – the modern holiday was first established in 1948. Coming of age ceremonies (*Seijin-shiki*) reflect both the expanded rights but also increased responsibilities expected of new adults and offer the opportunity to celebrate a family member's 'coming of age' if a formal celebration wasn't possible on the actual birth date. Give a gift of some family heirloom that signifies your recognition of their attaining maturity – which is, of course, eighteen or twenty-one in the West.

16 *Tokuwa no Tenjinsai*

In recognition of the scholars in the family starting back to school or university, offer up a prayer to Tenjin, the Japanese god of scholarship and learning – or his Western equivalent. And make a small 'good luck' gift to aid their studies.

February

In this season of intense cold, the flower that blossoms in the face of the frost and snow is the *utne* (*Prunus mume:* plum tree), which has been held in great esteem by the Japanese people from ancient times due to the length of the tree's life, the way in which the beautiful flowers unexpectedly come out from the old trunks having a charm of their own, the noble appearance of the blossoms, and the delicate fragrance which they emit in the depth of winter when nearly all other flowers are as yet asleep. The opening of the plum-blossoms may be said to be the first tidings of spring and the flower for February (*Floral Calendar of Japan*).

Many of the annual celebrations are fire festivals, just the same as folk-festivals in the West with a lead up to the beginning of spring.

1–2 February *Kurokawa Noh*

Ceremonial parades and seven sacred *noh* plays mark the beginning of the New Year, so why not restore the traditional family trip to the pantomime with a special high-tea or supper depending on the age of the guests?

2–4 February *Setsubun Mantoro*

At this twice-yearly festival in Nara, the shrine's thousands of stone lanterns as well as its famous bronze hanging lanterns are all lit to magical effect; there are believed to be over 3,000 of them in the shrine precincts, many of them evocatively covered in moss. They are lit twice a year during the nights of the Mantoro festivals in (*Setsubun*) February and (*Obon*) August. *Setsubun* is the day before the beginning of spring in Japan, and literally means 'seasonal division', but usually the term refers to the spring Setsubun, properly called *Risshun* celebrated yearly on 3 February as part of the Spring Festival, *Haru Matsuri*.

In its association with the Lunar New Year, spring *Setsubun* can be and was previously thought of as a sort of New Year's Eve celebration, and was accompanied by a special ritual to cleanse away all the evil of the former year and drive away disease-bringing evil spirits for the year to come. This special ritual is called *mamemaki* – literally 'bean scattering'). The head of the household (traditionally the father) would take roasted beans in his hand, pray at the family shrine, and then toss the sanctified beans out the door, while the family say: 'Demons out! Luck in!' and slam the door. Beans are also used to deflect ill-luck of negative energies throughout Europe and this celebration coincides with the traditional Western Candlemas and Imbolc observations.

9 February *O-tauesai*

This rice-planting festival is a Japanese celebration of fertility. After the rice-planting ceremony, a ritual dance simulates a couple having sexual intercourse. Masked goblins also hand out ritual smacks with bamboo sticks to 'drive the devil out'. Familiarise yourself with the spring planting traditions and customs from the county/country in which you live and inaugurate your own 'fruitful new beginnings' ritual.

12 February *Hatsu Uma* Festival

People pray for success in business to Inari (guardian of grains, especially rice and therefore business in general). Today, there is no need for a plentiful harvest since most people buy their food from the supermarket or via online shopping – but imagine what would happen if the *global* commercial growers suffered consecutive bad harvests. There would be a horror scenario of global proportions that would be a magnified problem of what our ancestors faced every single year of their lives! Offer a handful of rice to Inari.

19 February *Hachinohe Enburi*

This localised Japanese folk dance festival dates back to when people with no experience of farming were taught how to work in the fields through dancing. This is a good opportunity for a child's introduction to growing things.

March

On 3 March the people greet the *momo-no-sekku* (The Peach-blossom Festival), when their hearts swell with a feeling that it is really spring. The *momo-no-sekku* is also known as *hinamaturi* (The Doll Festival), and is a festival for young girls. What must never be lacking in this festival is one or two sprays of *momo* (*Prunus persica*: peach) inserted in a vase. This also is a custom dating from ancient times, and has become one of the regular observances of the month of March. The festival is held in order to bestow blessings upon young girls, and the peach, in this connection, is said to have the power of driving away devils (*Floral Calendar of Japan*).

These spring festivals are performed for the benefit of the family and can be seen as a personal welcome to the new growing year. From around the first of February on the island of Okinawa and the end of March to early May, cherry trees bloom all over Japan.

1–14 March *Todai-ji Shunie*

Festival of water and fire. Priests conduct a fire ceremony

every evening, swinging long torches in the air to ward off evil, while water is drawn from the 1200 year-old well and offered to visitors. Light outdoor lanterns to welcome the beginning of spring.

3 March *Nagashi-bina.*

An event that involves dispelling impurities and misfortunes by floating dolls away on water. In this rite, dry straw is woven into a boat, which carries a pair of male and female dolls to be cast adrift in the river. Girls float a pair of husband and wife dolls on the lid of a rice container together with some sweets to keep away misfortune and pray for good health. *Nagashibina* literally means 'doll floating' and refers to the ancient ritual, imported from Chinese Taoist and Yin-Yang theory (*onmyodo* in Japanese) which are at the heart of much of Japan's ancient Shinto practices. In the ritual, these small dolls made of straw were floated down a river and out to sea, and each doll carried the 'pollution' or 'sin' of the person each doll represented; not too dissimilar to the Jewish custom of scapegoating adopted in European cultures. Purity, and its antithesis – pollution in a spiritual sense – is at the heart of many Shinto rituals, and throwing things into a river to be carried away to the sea is a fairly common concept.

3 March *Hina Matsuri*

Girls' Day – also known as the Doll's Festival – is to pray for the health and happiness of young girls and marked by families displaying a set of traditional *hina* dolls (often family heirlooms) in the house and serving special food delicacies that are ceremonially beautiful and delicious. Traditionally, girls in Japan invited their friends to a home party to celebrate this festival – which is an idea that can be adopted in the West.

6 March *Otaue-sai*

A ceremonial rice planting festival to mark the beginning of spring and traditionally features time-honoured *kagura* dances and *bugaku* court music. Sow the first seeds of spring.

April

It is the *sakura* (cherry) that is the queen of flowers in April, and it is so representative of all flowers in Japan:

The cherries of Yosino have blossomed -
The flowers of spring that are like the supreme ruler

How right we think it is that the cherry should be the favourite flower of the Japanese, for its splendour when it blooms and for its gallantry when it falls (*Floral Calendar of Japan*).

Again the festivals are focusing on the well-being and harmony of the home and family

1–30 April. *Miyako Odori*

This is one of the four great spring shows in the five *geisha* districts (*hanamachi*) of Kyōto, Japan. The dances, songs, and theatre productions presented in the framework of the *Miyako Odori* are performed by the *maiko* and *geiko* of the Gion quarter. The motifs draw from classical Japanese culture and incorporate everyday life as well as folkloristic elements. A good time to support a local theatre production or concert for a family night out.

First Sunday in April *Obasama Festival*

A spring planting festival that was performed in the hope of a good harvest ahead of the spring farming period. Plant the first of the year's bedding plants or vegetables.

May

When the trees gradually begin to put on their summer attire, the leaves of the different trees first appear as a fresh, vivid green;

then little by little they acquire a beautiful glossiness, just as if they had been brought back to life again. The weather tells us that summer has already come, but the calendar calls this month *bansyun* ('late spring'). In Japanese poetical language the flowers of this month are known as *yokwai* ('the left-behind flowers'), and in fact *tutuzi* (azaleas), *huzi* (wistarias), *botan* (peonies), *kiri* (paulownias), and *honoki* and *taizanboku* (different kinds of magnolias) flower one after the other as if they were trying to make up for being late (*Floral Calendar of Japan*).

The beginning of May is also a time for all manner of localised festivals and celebrations including puppet plays, parades and processions, storytelling and a range of other classical arts and festival amusements – all in keeping with the Western traditions surrounding May Day.

1–3 May *Yotaka Matsuri*

At the pre-festival, *ando* (large, magnificent paper lantern sculptures) light up the night. Believed to have started in the Taisho Period c.1652 to welcome the shrine's *kami* and to ask for a bountiful harvest, decorative lanterns can be lit to accompany a request for prosperity.

5 May *Tango no Sekku*

This Boys' Festival has been celebrated for over a millennium and was originally celebrated in the houses of warriors because it honoured boys' courage and determination. Many of the symbols of this day are about having the character of a warrior and eventually this day became important to all households in Japan with boys. After WWII, Boys' Day was toned down and the holiday officially became known as Children's Day or **Kodomo no hi**. It was supposed to be a day to celebrate the health and happiness of all children but many still see it as Boys' Festival. For those with children it can be celebrated as you choose – see **3 March**.

8 May *Yoshida Jinja*

Offer prayers to the *kami* of cooking, eating and drinking. So celebrate with a home-cooked meal for friends and family.

Full Moon in May *Uesaku Festival*

Offer prayers to the *kami* for world peace with fires lit in the temple grounds.

June

Now, according to the calendar also, summer has really come. The earth is wholly covered with green, and all nature has put on its summer livery. It is in this month that, the grain harvest being over, water is run into the rice-fields, and the rice seedlings are planted. From about the middle of the month to about the middle of July warm, moist south-east winds blow from the Continent, and practically the whole of Japan is enveloped in the so-called *tuyu* or rainy season, during which we have spells of muggy, oppressive weather. The flower for this month is indubitably the *hanasyobu* (*Iris ensata, var. hortensis*: iris). This is a plant which is said to have originally grown wild in a small marsh in the mountains of north-eastern Japan, and that it was brought to Edo (the present Tokyo) some three hundred years ago and cultivated there. It is a perennial herbaceous plant belonging to the family of Iridaceae. Mention must be made of the *syobuta* (iris field) in the precincts of the Meizi Shrine, since it is the place where the *hanasyobu* is found in its greatest perfection (*Floral Calendar of Japan*).

June is the time for the major rice-planting festivals that date back more than 1700 years when women ritually plant rice seedlings in the paddy fields to the accompaniment of traditional music and rice-planting folk songs. This event was symbolically used at the end of the famous Akira Kurosawa film, *Seven Samurai,* with great effect.

Early-Mid June *Chagu-Chagu Umakko* (Horse Festival)

The Morioka region of northern Japan is famous for its horses and this festival was originally conceived by horse breeders who wished to pray for long and happy lives for their animals. It now features a parade of colourfully dressed horses ridden by local children with round 80–100 horses usually taking part dressed in *konida* costumes (worn by the horses of *daimyo* – feudal lords – in the Edo Period). The name of the festival comes from the noise made by the bells (*chagu chagu*) on the horses' harnesses (*umakko*) and the event is designated as a national intangible folklore cultural asset. At the end of the parade, prayers are offered for a bountiful rice harvest and thanks are given to the horses.

July

Early on July mornings to stand by the edge of a pond and watch the lotus flowers open is an unforgettable summer experience. The *hasn* (*Nelumbo nucifera*: lotus) was originally a native of tropical Asia, but it has been cultivated in Japan from ancient times, and is seen growing in abundance in ponds in the gardens of temples and private residences (*Floral Calendar of Japan*).

July is the month for celebrating numerous fire festivals and folk traditions

6–8 July *Iriya no Asagao-ichi*

Iriya (morning glories) flowers are said to symbolise the beginning of summer and bring good luck. Every year, thousands come to the Kishibojin Temple area to buy morning glory plants from hundreds of street stalls. Plant the flower in the garden or large pots to act as your own annual symbol of summer.

August

The favourite flower for this month has been from ancient times the *asagao* (*Pharbitis Nil*: morning glory). Though the garden be, as they say in Japanese, 'as narrow as a cat's forehead', if only the homeowner sets up this pot of morning glory in it and it blooms, they can appreciate the beauty of summer. The morning glory's original home is in tropical regions, but in China there are records of its use as a medicinal plant 2,200 years ago, and it was introduced into Japan about a thousand years ago. As the morning glory has long been loved by the Japanese, it appears in many paintings and poems (*uta* and *haiku*) but because of its homeliness and its close association with the life of the common people, it does not often occur as the main theme, but is usually added as one of the natural features of the season (*Floral Calendar of Japan*).

The observances for this month are focused upon the ancestors and Otherworld activities similar to Hallowe'en in the West.

13–16 August *Obon Mantoro*

Obon (or *Bon*) is a Japanese Buddhist custom to honour the spirits of the ancestors. This Buddhist-Confucian custom has evolved into a family reunion holiday during which people return to ancestral family places and visit and clean their ancestors' graves, and when the spirits of the ancestors are supposed to revisit the household altars. It has been celebrated in Japan for more than 500 years and traditionally includes a dance, known as *Bon-Odori*. *Kyū Bon* (Old Bon) is celebrated on the fifteenth day of the seventh month of the lunar calendar, and so differs each year.

Among the traditional preparations for the ancestors' return is the cleaning of grave sites. The welcoming fire (*mukaebi*) built on the thirteenth and the send-off fire (*okuribi*) built on the fifteenth and sixteenth are intended to light the path. Families sent their ancestor's spirits back to their permanent dwelling place under the guidance of fire: this latter rite was known as 'sending fire' and the closing of the festival. One traditional custom to mark the end of the Bon Festival is the lighting of small paper lanterns containing a burning flame that are either set afloat on a river, lake or sea, or let go and float away into the night. Their light is intended to guide the way for deceased family members' spirits to return to Otherworld.

Toro Nagashi is a symbol of summer with the soothing beauty of paper lanterns floating along the tranquil Sumida-gawa River and as *Obon* occurs in the heat of the summer, participants traditionally wear yukata, or lightweight cotton kimonos. This activity is traditionally performed on the final evening of the Bon and is a hauntingly beautiful sight; the peaceful custom is a gesture of respect for those who have passed away and gives participants a moment to think about their ancestors, loved ones or even past pets. The three-day Buddhist Obon festival is held in honour of one's ancestors; *Toro Nagashi* is meant to be more of a joyful celebration than a time of mourning.

September

Gathering the flowers blooming in the autumn fields —
When we count them
their kinds are seven.

This is a poem written a thousand years ago, and from ancient times seven flowers, known as *aki no nanakusa* or 'the seven herbs of autumn', have been taken as the representatives of all autumn flowers, and have been much used as subjects of poetry and painting. All are plain, homely flowers, without the least trace of gaudiness. They are: *hagi* (*Lespedeza spp*: bush clover); *susuki* (Miscanthus sinensis: pampas grass); *kuzu* (*Pueraria Thunbergiana, var typica*: arrowroot); *nadesiko* (Dianthus superbus: pink); *ominaesi* (*Patrinia scabiosaefolia*: golden lace flower); *huzibakama* (*Eupatorium japonicum*: aster), and *kikyo* (*Platycodon glaucum*: bell flower) (*Floral Calendar of Japan*).

At this time of the year, graveyards in Japan will be densely covered in bizarrely shaped crimson flowers brightly glistening in the autumn sun. That's the *higanbana* – red spider lily (*Lycoris radiate*) and the best way to enjoy their dark beauty is on a sunny, autumn day's stroll through the rice paddies at *O-higan*, where the deep red flowers growing alongside the bright yellow rice fields ready for harvest make for a colourful contrast. Rice farmers don't put them there solely for aesthetic reasons, though. As with any amaryllis, their bulbs are poisonous and they are supposed to keep moles, mice and other hole-digging vermin that might damage the crops, at bay.

O-higan

This the day of the Autumn Equinox and it's a national holiday in Japan because from this day on (23 September to be correct), the dark of night will become longer than the day-light period and it's time to get serious about the ghosts that haunt the long winter nights. Traditionally it is a time to take care of the unruly, potentially vengeful souls of the ancestors since *higan* translates as the 'other shore' – the land of the dead. Thus *o-higan* is the day to visit the family graves and to pray for the well-being of the departed souls; where old countryside graveyards will be densely covered with these bizarrely shaped crimson flowers like violently shed blood rising straight out of the ground. Why not plant three or four bulbs in a large plot so that they bloom in time for the Autumn Equinox.

October

October is a month for fruits rather than for flowers. Apples, grapes, figs, kaki (persimmons), and chestnuts are the most important (*Floral Calendar of Japan*).

The Autumn Harvest Festivals are celebrated around the time of the rice harvest to thank the gods for a bountiful crop. There is no exact date, since it is varied and is only celebrated in the month of October.

Momijigari

Just as the *sakura* or cherry blossom represents spring, the *momiji* or autumn leaves, have traditionally represented autumn in Japan, and the pleasurable pastime of viewing autumn colours is called *momiji-gari*, which literally means 'hunting the autumn leaves'. Japanese people enjoy *momiji-gari*, which is regarded as a seasonal event equally as important as *hanami*, or flower viewing, and both practices are deeply rooted in their lives. Originally the practice of viewing autumn colours is thought to have started off as an elegant pastime mainly enjoyed by the court and aristocracy in the seventh century. That changed, however, around the seventeenth century during the Edo period, when the custom spread to commoners and people began to hold *sake* parties and sumptuous feasts while viewing the beautiful autumn landscapes.

In general, the use of the term *momiji* is applied to all deciduous trees that produce autumnal leaves toned with a red or yellow, including maple, the Japanese lacquer tree, and the ginkgo. The term has also come to be used to represent the maple, the actual name for which is Kaede, because of the particular beauty of the leaves. There are many Japanese *tanka* and *haiku* poems about the autumn leaves and the joys of viewing them. The *momiji* tradition has also found expression in the *noh* and *kabuki* theatrical forms; *kimono* and *obi* sashes have also incorporated special traditional autumn motifs.

Like the cherry blossom, the *momiji* reaches its peak in a rather short time and then fades and drops off the tree. It represents delicate short-lived beauty that Japanese people are traditionally fond of, like a samurai, who has lived a short but honourable life. Autumn leaves peak and then fall, followed by the first snows of winter, completing the natural life cycle that Japanese have experienced for centuries. Make a habit of viewing this 'season of mists and mellow fruitfulness' wherever you can find it – and take the time to stand and stare.

November

The mountains become gay for a while with red and yellow hues; of flowers there is only the chrysanthemum to give colour to autumn as it dies. But the red foliage (*momizi*) of the trees and the chrysanthemums are able by themselves to make both the country and the garden as beautiful as did all the hundred flowers of spring. Places noted for their momizi or chrysanthemums are crowded with people, for November offers the last chance for outings in the year. Just as the cherry is considered to be the queen of flowers in spring, so the chrysanthemum is to be regarded as the queen of flowers in autumn. The crest of the Japanese Imperial Family is a chrysanthemum flower and as such is revered by the whole nation (*Floral Calendar of Japan*).

The beginning of November is the time for historical costume street parades, with festivals of dance and music to give thanks for the harvest, and a time to pray for family prosperity. It is also a time for a sacred fire ritual to banish evil spirits and anticipating the coming of winter with *kagura* dances, thundering *taiko* drums and bonfires celebrating the time when the gods landed on the earth.

December

We have finally reached the last month of the year, which, according to the Japanese calendar, is the first month of winter. *Tya-no-hana* (tea blossoms) and *sazanka* (*Camellia sasanqua*) are about the only flowers of this month. *Tya-no-hana* is the blossom of the famous Japanese green tea, and is white and very lovely; the blossoms have five petals and long yellow stamens. The leaves are gathered in May. The *sazanka* bears a resemblance to the camellia (*tubaki*), but it is quieter in appearance. The flowers are pale pink or white. It is cultivated in gardens, and is used for making hedges; in the south of Japan it is found growing wild (*Floral Calendar of Japan*).

13 December Preparation for the New Year

Preparations for seeing in the New Year were originally undertaken to greet the *toshigami*, or deity of the incoming year. These began on 13 December, when the house was given a thorough cleaning; the date is usually nearer the end of the month now. The house is then decorated in the traditional fashion: a sacred rope of straw (*shimenawa*) with dangling white paper strips (*shide*) is hung over the front door to prevent evil spirits from entering and to show the presence of the *toshigami*. It is also customary to place *kadomatsu*, an arrangement of tree sprigs, beside the entrance way. This is in preparation for the New Year holidays. Decorations and sundry goods are sold at the local fair. Originally these year-end fairs provided opportunities for farmers, fisher-folk and mountain dwellers to exchange goods and buy clothes and other necessities for the coming year.

All cultures have their heroes and there are usually calendar days set aside to honour them, which are an important part of remembering our history and cultural heritage. For example:

14 December: The revenge of the forty-seven *rōnin*

Also known as the Akō incident – is an eighteenth-century historical event in Japan in which a band of *rōnin* (leaderless samurai) avenged the death of their master. The story tells of a group of samurai who were left leaderless after their *daimyō* (feudal lord) Asano Naganori was compelled to perform *seppuku* (ritual suicide) for assaulting a court official named Kira Yoshinaka. After waiting and planning for a year, the *rōnin* avenged their master's honour by killing Kira. In turn, they were themselves obliged to commit *seppuku* for committing the crime of murder. This true story was popularized in Japanese culture as emblematic of the loyalty, sacrifice, persistence, and honour that people should preserve in their daily lives. Each year in December, Sengakuji Temple, where Asano Naganori and the *rōnin* are buried, holds a festival commemorating the legendary event. There is a classic Kenji Mizoguchi film version of the story entitled *The 47 Ronin.*

31 December Ōmisoka

People do the general house cleaning (Ōsōji) to welcome the coming year and not to keep having impure influences. Many people visit Buddhist temples to hear the temple bells rung 108 times at midnight (*joya no kane*) to announce the passing of the old year and the coming of the new. The reason they are rung 108 times is because of the Buddhist belief that human beings are plagued by 108 earthly desires or passions (*bonnō*) and with each ring, one desire is dispelled. It is also a custom to eat *toshikoshi-soba* in the hope that the family fortunes will extend like the long noodles.

It should be obvious from the small selection of festivals mentioned above that the Japanese do – and always have – placed great emphasis on showing reverence for their ancestors and cultural heritage, while some tend to be more devoted to family participation. Even if we are not taking part in any religious tradition, we still need to observe certain personal devotions in order to make a statement of who we are – even if it's only for ourselves.

When things flourish they begin to decline
At midday the sun starts to set
When the moon is done waxing
It starts to wane.

The Kensho Moment: Exercise

At the turning points of the year in spring and autumn, if we focus our attention on the wonders of Nature, we are also synchronising with the various folk-traditions for both East and West. These are the times when the changing natural tides influence spiritual and mystical matters all over the world.

Vernal Equinox (*Shunbun no Hi*) is a public holiday in Japan, usually 20–21 March, although the date of the holiday is not officially declared until February of the previous year, due to the need for astronomical measurements. Vernal Equinox Day became a public holiday in 1948 and prior to that it was the spring date of *Shunki kōreisai* dedicated to the imperial ancestors and to the *kami* collectively. Like other Japanese holidays, this holiday was repackaged as a non-religious holiday for the sake of separation of religion and state in Japan's post-war constitution.

- This is the time for observation and silent contemplation in a natural landscape; ideally while 'flower viewing'.

Yet **Summer Solstice**, or *Geshi* as it's called in Japan, passes relatively unnoticed except for the ritual bathing in the sea to purify body and soul as the sun comes up between a pair of sacred rocks known as Meotoiwa. This ritual *Geshisai* takes place at daybreak every year at Ise – famous for being the home of Ise Jingu, the most sacred Shinto shrine in Japan representing as they do, the union of Izanagi and Izanami, the two Shinto gods responsible for the creation of the Islands of Japan. The sunrise is seen just at the midpoint of the two rocks for one week before and after the solstice; only during these weeks, the sun appears to come up from behind Mt. Fuji in the far distance, if the weather permits – but the chances of seeing beautiful sunrises there are not high because it is in the middle of the rainy season! This small shrine with one of its *torii* gates standing offshore is a popular tourist attraction. Meotoiwa is actually the shrine gate for the divine stone *Okitama Shinseki* located underwater about 700 metres offshore, which is said to be a holy rock, of the god of entertainment, Sarutahiko no Ookami.

- Make a point of getting up early to watch the sunrise – even if it's only from the bedroom window with a cup of tea – and bathe in the morning glow.

On 22, 23 or 24 September the **Autumnal Equinox** is celebrated as a national holiday in Japan and known as *Shubun-no-hi*. The exact day can vary due to astronomical observations, so the date for the following year is usually announced in early spring. This was originally known as the Autumn Commemoration for the Imperial Spirits (*Shuki koreisai*).

- Legend has it that the scent of the red spider lily (*higanbana*) will bring back all the beautiful memories of the dead for one last time, before they disappear when they cross the Forgotten River. And their blooming represents the changing from summer to autumn. The transient beauty of the flower recalls those who have departed from this life but live on in our memory.

Even the **Winter Solstice**, *Tōji*, does not go unmarked in Japan, even if it is small-scale – the most well-known activity is taking a bath with a type of citrus called *yuzu* in the water. Although the power of the sun is weakest at this time of the year, it becomes stronger from this day and it is said that the fortune of people rise from this day.

- Find a peaceful place to watch the sunset on this shortest of days and wait quietly for owl-light to descend to create that 'time between times' so familiar to those pagans in the West.

Be empty, be still
Watch everything
Just come and go.

Chapter Four

The Meditation Garden

To watch the sun sink behind a flower clad hill.
To wander on in a huge forest without thought of return.
To stand upon the shore and gaze after a boat that disappears behind
distant islands.
To contemplate the flight of wild geese seen and lost among the
clouds.
And, subtle shadows of bamboo on bamboo.
Zeami Motokiyo

In the BBC series, *The Art of Japanese Life*, Dr James Fox visited the famous Ryoan-ji Zen garden at the Temple of the Dragon at Peace. The Ryōan-ji garden is considered one of the finest surviving examples of *kare-sansui* or 'dry landscape'. A refined type of Zen temple garden design generally featuring distinctive larger rock formations arranged amidst a sweep of smooth pebbles (small, carefully selected polished river rocks) raked into linear patterns that facilitate meditation, since the garden is meant to be viewed from a seated position on the veranda of the *hōjō*, the residence of the abbot of the monastery.

The enclosed garden is a rectangle of twenty-five by ten metres and placed within it are fifteen stones of different sizes, carefully composed in five groups; one group of five stones, two groups of three, and two groups of two stones. The stones are surrounded by white gravel, which is carefully raked each day by the monks. The only vegetation in the garden is some moss around the stones that are placed so that the entire composition cannot be seen at once from the veranda; they are arranged so that when looking at the garden from any angle (other than from above) only fourteen of the boulders are visible at any one time.

It is traditionally said that only through attaining enlightenment would one be able to view the fifteenth boulder and acts as a reminder of human imperfection – that one mind cannot understand everything.

The wall enclosing the garden is an important element of the whole. It is made of clay, which has been stained by age with subtle brown and orange tones and when it was restored in 1977, the tile roof of the wall was replaced with tree bark to give it back its original appearance. Not everyone, of course, can visit this fabled garden but as part of *Japanese Gardens* – from the Ambient DVD Collection – there is a sequence filmed on a rainy day at Ryoan-ji with just the sound of rain falling and flowing along the drainage channels. It brings home the tranquillity and contemplative quality of this sacred place and without being aware of it, the ambiance draws the viewer in ...

Like any work of art, the artistic garden of Ryōan-ji has been dissected and analysed hundreds of times in an attempt to discover its meaning – from islands in a foaming ocean, to swimming baby tigers, to the peaks of mountains rising above clouds, to theories about secrets of geometry, or of the rules of equilibrium of odd numbers. Garden historian Gunter Nitschke wrote: 'The garden at Ryōan-ji does not symbolize anything, or more precisely, to avoid any misunderstanding, the garden of Ryōan-ji does not symbolize, nor does it have the value of reproducing a natural beauty that one can find in the real or mythical world. I consider it to be an abstract composition of "natural" objects in space, a composition whose function is to incite meditation.'

During Dr Fox's contemplatory visit, he found that as time passes something remarkable happens: the gaps between the stones come alive and the emptiness fills up with a vast panorama of the world – then, just like that, it is nothing more than group of rocks. 'If this garden has a meaning it is something that ultimately comes from within ourselves – this garden is a blank canvas that allows the mind to wander.'

This strange experience is intrinsically Japanese and summed up as *'ma'* – a word that can be roughly translated as 'gap', 'space', 'pause' or 'the space between two structural parts'. *Ma* is not something that is created by compositional elements; it takes place in the imagination of the human who experiences these elements and can be defined as experiencing the understanding of place with emphasis on the 'interval'. In Japanese, *ma*, the word for space, suggests interval. 'It is best described as a consciousness of place, not in the sense of an enclosed three-dimensional entity, but rather the simultaneous awareness of form and non-form deriving from an intensification of vision. *Ma* is the emptiness full of possibilities, like a promise yet to be fulfilled.'

Far from being just a philosophical or artistic concept, however, *ma* is ever-present in all aspects of Japanese daily life – the pure, and indeed essential, void between all 'things'. As a small example, a tea break in a busy day has to be in a quiet place, away from the work routine – giving the opportunity to soak in the serenity of *ma* before getting back to busy life. In our own busy lives, it is easy to feel there is not enough time to do everything properly but no matter how little time we can devote to any task, it has to have a deliberate beginning and a deliberate end, albeit short. Otherwise, our time goes by filled with one thing after another, like an essay with a lot of words – without complete sentences, paragraphs, commas and full stops. When Japanese are taught to bow in early age, they are told to make a deliberate pause at the end of the bow before they come back up – to make sure there is enough *ma* in their bow for it to have meaning and look respectful.

Ma is manifest in all aspects of Japanese living – architecture, garden design, music, art, theatre, flower arrangements (*ikebana*) and poetry because where there is clutter even valuable things lose their value. Where there is too much, nothing stands out when a home is cluttered with disordered things that impede movement or reduce effectiveness; similar in essence to *feng shui* the Chinese metaphysical and quasi-philosophical system that seeks to harmonize individuals with their surrounding environment. When we feel there is too much clutter, it is not because we have too many things; it is rather because we don't have enough *ma*. The presence of *ma* makes the minimalism of a Japanese *tatami* room so serene but whereas minimalism is limited to physical form and space, *ma* is not.

The awareness of *ma* is what makes minimalism possible; *ma* is in the purposeful pause in speech which make words stand out. It is in the quiet time we all need to make our busy lives meaningful, and in the silence between the notes which make the music. *Ma* is what creates the peace of mind (called *heijoshin* in Japanese) we all need, so that there is room for our thoughts to exist properly, and to thrive.

Ma is possibly best described by what we would define in the West as 'elbow room' or breathing space because it is like a frame within which things can exist, stand out and have meaning. If someone is arranging a display of any kind, they may say that a certain piece needs 'more elbow room' in order to show it off to its best advantage. Similarly, artists understand the importance of this 'negative space' which surrounds an object in an image because its use can have a dramatic impact on the mood and tone of the finished work. Negative space is the space around and between the subject(s) of an image and may be most evident when the space around a subject, not the subject itself, forms an interesting or artistically relevant shape, and such space occasionally is used to artistic effect as the 'real' subject of an image. *Ma* takes the concept of negative space further, to define that which spans both space and time – as within the arrangement of stones or flowers.

Or in simpler terms, as in Sei Shonagon's *Pillow Book*, we can see how the pause between each seasonal cameo stands out from the rest of the text to create a framed image within our mind's eye:

In the spring it is the dawn that is the most beautiful As the light creeps over the hyacinth shaded hills, their outlines are dyed a faint red and wisps of purplish cloud trail over them.

In summer the nights. Not only when the moon shines, but on dark nights, too, as the fireflies flit to and fro, and even when it rains, how beautiful it is!

In autumn the evenings, when the glittering sun sinks close to the edge of the hills and the crows fly back to their nests in threes and fours and twos; more charming still is a file of wild geese, like specks in the distant sky. When the sun has set, one's heart is moved by the sound of the wind and the hum of the insects.

In winter the early mornings. It is beautiful indeed when snow has fallen during the night, but splendid too when the ground is white with frost; or even if there is no snow or frost but it is simply very cold and the attendants hurry from room to room stirring up the fires and bringing charcoal, how well it fits the season's mood. But as noon approaches and the cold wears off, no one bothers to keep the braziers alight, and soon nothing remains but piles of white ashes.

The Sacred Space

Again, few of us have the space to create a traditional Japanese garden but we should bear in mind that if it's big enough to sit in, then there's room to meditate. It's the ambiance of the space surrounding us that is important – not the space itself.

Tsuboniwa or the courtyard garden was originally designed for the interior spaces of Heian period palaces, and were intended to give a glimpse of nature and some privacy to the residents of the rear side of the building. They were as small as one *tsubo*, or about 3.3 square metres. During the Edo period, merchants began building small gardens in the space behind their shops, which faced the street, and their residences, located at the rear. These tiny gardens were meant to be seen, not entered, and usually had a stone lantern, a water basin, stepping stones and a few plants. Today, *tsuboniwa* are found in many Japanese residences, hotels, restaurants, and public buildings.

Because of the limited space available for an authentic Japanese garden, I have created a *tsuboniwa* in a small enclosed area between the back of the house and the boundary hedge, following the instructions of Kiyoshi Seike in *A Japanese Touch for Your Garden*:

> The gardener does not fill it up; this would only congest it. Instead he carefully arranges a few items and uses their relationships to suggest more than is immediately visible to the eye. He adds manmade items like lanterns and *tsukubai* (water basins) to humanise the garden, to decorate it, and to allow it to function practically in daily life. He aims for balance and proportion without resorting to geometric artifice. He links the garden compositionally to his home. And he exploits numerous untouchables: wind direction, sounds, seasons, sunlight, the true and apparent dimensions of empty space.

We can, however, build a *tsuboniwa* in the smallest of spaces. The courtyard garden is perfect for Western town dwelling-spaces because of the irregular areas between properties, small back yards, narrow alleyways, shady basement areas and balconies. All of these areas can be cleverly converted to a peaceful meditational space where the individual can retreat for a moment; or designed to link the outside space to the inside of the home for the delectation of the eye with the subtle use of lighting. Using the Zen approach – of simplicity in design and attention to detail – is useful in a small garden. An illusion of space can be created by leaving as much as two-thirds of the space plain gravel and then adding an aesthetically pleasing arrangement on which to focus the eye.

Even these tiny gardens, however, are not designed to be static. In the spring it should burst into colour and begin growing; in winter it should still be a place of repose. Sometimes the gardener adds his own personal touch to match the mood of the year and in doing so celebrates the flow of nature. For example:

- **Spring**: Pots that contain forsythia or dwarf iris are disguised by baskets to suggest that the plant actually grows in the garden.
- **Summer**: A scarlet or brightly coloured umbrella against the greenery helps to 'cool' the garden on a hot day. A lazy smoke rising from a mosquito smudge gives the impression of summer.
- **Autumn**: Chrysanthemums do not grow wild in nature; unlike the spring forsythia, their ceramic pots should be left exposed to view.
- **Winter**: Sprinkled with snow the garden is reduced to its bare essentials.

So ... here we have four different seasonal outlooks with the minimum amount of fuss that is the complete antithesis to the traditional English cottage garden with its multitude of different coloured flowers and shrubs, all mixed together in a kaleidoscope of texture, hues, shades and perfumes. The rest of my garden is like that ... but my private space is stripped down to the bare bones ... this is where I get away from it all, hail, rain or shine at any time of the year, day or night ... because this indoor/outdoor space has been designed that way.

Regardless of size, the first step is to strip everything out so all that is left is the blank canvas against which we can place the items we want to include – keeping in mind the importance of balance and proportion. Although traditional temple Zen gardens use white gravel (or sand) as a foundation, brownish-grey gravel is more often used in private gardens and often chosen to conceal drainage pipes and drain covers. Any walls should be painted off-white or concealed with lengths of split bamboo (*misu-gaki*) to create the appearance of a screen.

Neutral coloured pots can be used for planting and obtained in sets of four or five from a local garden centre; use the largest for bamboo since this plant is particularly invasive if left to its own devices. Plant the smaller ones with azalea, forsythia and dwarf iris for spring and early summer blooming because the pots can be moved around to catch the sun, or take a back seat when not in flower. Lanterns and water basins can also be purchased locally and made from reconstituted stone – painted with natural yoghurt these will weather quite nicely in their first year. A small balcony or terrace may only need an azalea, three different sized stones and an ornamental figure to produce a subtle Zen corner; and pots – like stones – should always be in groups of one, two, three or five.

Surprisingly enough, the oldest surviving gardening book is *Sakuteiki* from the Heian period that opens with the words: *Ishi wo taten kota* – 'The art of setting stones'. This tells us right from the beginning that it is stones themselves that are the important focal point of the Japanese garden. We understand from it that the simple act of standing a stone upright was so spiritually and aesthetically powerful that it became central to the process of making a garden; the act of setting the stones became an appellation for gardening itself. According to a new translation of an eleventh-century text, the importance placed on stones in Japan stems from several sources.

The first is the ancient use of stones as prayer sites, especially those found naturally in the landscape, often stones that have a rounded form or a naturally upright appearance. It was believed that through the medium of the stone, gods could be induced to descend from their heavenly abode to visit earth and bestow their blessings for good health and ample harvests on village communities. These sacred stones, called *iwakura*, are still actively incorporated in religious life even today.

In later eras, the spiritual qualities inherent in sacred stones carried over into the use of stones in manmade gardens. New meanings were added but the belief that the setting of the stones was central to the art of gardening, that the stones were animate objects and that the desires of the stones warranted consideration. But not just any old stones are used in Japanese gardens. Uncut stones that show the effects of weathering are favoured and have special qualities related to the areas from which they came; they may have been roughed or smoothed by rivers or oceans, or been eaten away by violent winds and storms. Their colour may have been enhanced to give calmness and stability; and rocks with growths of rust or moss are especially prized.

In very small gardens think about creating a grouping of three stones called *sanzon*, representing the Buddhist trinity – it is a triangular grouping with one tall central stone and two smaller ones flanking it for balance. While the stones should all be of different sizes, it is important that they are all the same colour to create harmony. Even if the grouping is the main point of interest, it should be placed a bit off to the side rather than in the centre. The stones should look as though they've been there forever with plantings around the bases to soften the bareness of the rock. If in full sun, the plants will need plenty of water in summer to prevent their taking the stones' radiant heat.

The *Sakuteiki* also reflects the superstitions concerning the many taboos that are an integral part of the placing of stones:

'If so much as one of these taboos is violated, the master of the household will fall ill and eventually die, and his land will fall into desolation and become the abode of devils.' It can best be described as the eighth-century Japanese *feng shui* of gardening, since it also calls upon that 'invisible energy' that binds the universe, earth, and humanity together, known as *ki*. Examples of some of those ancient taboos are as follows:

- Using a stone that once stood upright in a reclining manner or using a reclining stone as a standing stone. If this is done, that stone will definitely become a Phantom Stone and be cursed.
- Do not set a stone that is higher than the veranda in the immediate vicinity of the house. If this rule is not obeyed, trouble, and the master of the household will not live for long. However, temples and shrines that are exempt from this rule will follow one after another
- Stones inhabited by vengeful spirits always land the right way up if they fall from a height. Such stones should not be used. Throw them away!

Before making a start, obtain a number of books on Japanese garden design – classic and modern – and draw up a plan of the space to be used. Discard any ideas that will make the garden appeared cluttered – remember *ma* – and obtain the stone(s) that are to be the main feature. Once you have them on site, play around with ideas and positioning until they feel 'right' because as strange as it may sound, stones do have a right way and a wrong way! Once the stones are in position, then you can decide on whether there is room, or the necessity, to add a lantern or sculpture, but once it all settles down you can sit and listen to the stones grow …

Water also has a deep symbolic meaning for the Japanese but its inclusion in the courtyard garden is a lot more subtle. The usual feature is the *tsukubai*, or water basin for ritual cleansing, complete with a bamboo ladle and stand. In the Zen garden, water is of such importance that even in the *kare-san* (dry garden) maintaining the illusion of its presence is of paramount importance. As Jenny Hendy explains in *Zen in Your Garden*, water is mutable, taking the shape of any container into which it is poured. This is symbolic of what Zen teaches about being open, not rigid in our thinking.

Water challenges our perception of reality and is paradoxical in nature. In winter, water will sometimes change its character completely to become ice. But ice and water are merely different states of the same element, just as life and death are both natural states of our human existence. You can occasionally see the bottom of a pool, but at other times the surface acts like a mirror and the water appears solid. Reflected objects look as though they are in the water, but of course this is just an illusion. It is water's ability to produce either a true of distorted image that explains its tremendous symbolic significance in Zen.

The traditional water basin must be kept clean and clear at all times, especially during the autumn and winter when water can quickly become stagnant and the Zen purity lost. Alternatively, we can use a reflecting bowl that mirrors its surroundings on the surface of the water. When the mind is free of thoughts and emotions, it too reflects an undistorted image. Remember, however, that water will take the shape of any vessel that it is put into, and, according to that shape, becomes good or bad.

If we look at the classic Japanese gardens from a Westerner's point of view, the first thing we probably notice is the lack of formal flower beds and yet there is no lack of colour. In spring the cherry blossom veil the mountains in a pale pink haze and swathes of indigo iris flank the pool; and while scarlet and pink azalea can cover large tracts of ground, the russet tones of the acer break up the greenery. Flowers are seen as Nature intended: as accessories to the landscape. Formal flower arrangements are intended for the home or temple not in the garden.

But flowers do play an important part in enhancing daily life. *Hanakotoba* is the Japanese form of the language of flowers, and in this practice, plants were given codes and passwords. Physiological effects and action under the colour of the flowers, put into words from the impressions of nature and the presence of thorns with the height of tall plants, flowers and garlands of flowers through the various types. These are meant to convey emotion and communicate directly to the recipient or viewer without needing the use of words ... for example:

- **Amaryllis** – Shy
- **Ambrosia** – Pious
- **Anemone** - Sincere
- **Aster** – Remembrance
- **Azalea** – Patient/Modest

Here the idea of good and evil fortune governs both the selection of material and the form of arrangement. A love affair might flounder on a poor choice of communication where everything had to be perfect – the calligraphy, ink, paper, the way it was folded, the flower attached to it ... In her *Pillow Book*, Sei Shonagon refers to a poem being sent to her, 'attached to some of the white blossom of the *u- no hana* (deutzia), and the paper was as white as the flower' and on another occasion 'a letter written on fine green paper is attached to a budding willow branch'.

Flowers are everywhere in Japanese culture and are used to set the mood during tea, welcome the New Year and pay respect to the dearly departed; they are like mirrors to the seasons, reflecting the passage of time. Here are some ways the Japanese use flowers for everyday and special celebrations.

- *Chabana* is a special presentation of flowers for tea. It includes branches and twigs from the surrounding area, along with seasonal blooms. It is often hung in a bamboo vase. The *chabana* is thought to establish a connection with nature and connect the ceremonial tearoom to the surrounding land.

- **Kadomatsu** is a floral arrangement made from bamboo and pine placed outside the door to celebrate the coming of the New Year. It is thought to welcome the gods to the home and promote health and happiness during the upcoming year.
- **Funeral Flowers**: Funerals are somber occasions in Japanese culture and follow a strict protocol. While flowers are included in the ceremony, some guidelines must be followed. Brightly coloured flowers are considered offensive for a funeral; flower colour should be subdued and never vivid. Like colour, fragrance should also be avoided in funeral flowers. The white chrysanthemum is the preferred funeral flower as it lacks both colour and fragrance.

The colours of some flowers are also considered unlucky. Red flowers, which are sometimes used at funerals (ie. *higanbana*) are undesirable not only for that reason but also because red is supposed to suggest the red flames of a fire. An odd number of flowers is lucky, while even numbers are unlucky and therefore undesirable, and never used in flower arrangements. With the odd numbers one avoids symmetry and equal balance, which are actually seldom found in nature, and which from the Japanese standpoint are never attractive in art of any description.

Ikebana is the Japanese art of flower arrangement; also known as *Kadō* (the 'way of flowers'), plants also play an important role in the native Shinto religion. *Yorishiro* are objects that divine spirits are summoned to; evergreen plants such as *kadomatsu* are a traditional decoration of the New Year placed in pairs in front of homes to welcome ancestral spirits or *kami* of the harvest; the pastime of viewing plants and appreciating flowers throughout the four seasons was established in Japan early on. The *ikebana* tradition, however, dates back to the seventh century when floral offerings were made at altars. Later, they were placed in the *tokonoma* (alcove) of a home. *Ikebana* reached its first zenith in the sixteenth century under the influence of the tea-masters and has grown over the centuries, with over 1,000 different schools in Japan and abroad.

Kadō is counted as one of the three classical Japanese arts of refinement, along with *kōdō* for incense appreciation and *chadō* for tea and the tea ceremony. The idea of good and evil fortune governs both the selection of material and the form of arrangement, since the Japanese give an expression of the seasons in their floral arrangements, grouping the flowers differently according to the time of the year. For example, in the month of March, when high winds prevail, the unusual curves of the branches convey at once the impression of strong winds. In summer the Japanese rejoice in the low, broad receptacles, where the visually predominating water produces a cooler and more refreshing arrangement than those in upright vases. There is no occasion which cannot be suggested by the manner in which the flowers are arranged.

There are appropriate arrangements for all felicitous occasions, as well as for sad ones. An offering at death should be of white flowers, with some dead leaves and branches, so arranged as to express peace. All gifts of flowers must be in bud, so that the person to whom they are sent may have the pleasure of seeing them open – quite a contrast to the present Western idea of everything being forced to perfection before leaving the florist. The spiritual aspect of *kadō* is considered very important to its practitioners. Some practitioners feel silence is needed while making *ikebana* while others feel this is not necessary.

This idea of spiritual enlightenment through concentration and practice is central to the Zen philosophy. For many of its practitioners, *ikebana* is a lifelong lesson, a way to achieve a little inner stillness in which to work towards a richer spiritual understanding of the world, just like the Zen monks do through their meditation techniques. But how does *ikebana* help people develop their spirituality? The best answers to this can be found in the classic text, *Rikka-Imayo-Sugata* (1688), which is well known for its first usage of the term, *Kado,* and lists the ten virtues of a true 'Ikebana Master'.

No discrimination: Nature does not discriminate; neither should the *ikebana* practitioner. Through contemplating the capacity of nature to just exist, we learn to interact with all people and all things equally.

Selfless mind: When we face flowers, we are free from any concerns and we can clear our minds. The first goal of Zen meditation is to achieve such a clear mind, free from the chattering self. This first step is often the hardest for any student of meditation but with the help of the natural elements in their arrangements, many *ikebana* students come to experience this state of mind almost without realising it.

Making friends without words: Facing flowers, we feel a joy beyond words. When we share this joy with other people, we can form a bond that transcends language. Through our arrangements we can communicate on a deeper level with people no matter what language they speak.

Learn plants: *Ikebana* helps us learn about many kinds of flowers and trees with very little effort. We learn their names and we become in tune with the nature of each plant and its cycle. In particular, we learn how short the life of a flower is. This in turn, makes us realise how short our life is. Once we realize that our life, as well as our desire, is transient, it's easy to develop negative attitudes, to start thinking that life itself is meaningless. But through the simple beauty of a flower, so content with the nature of its own short life, we can come to appreciate the transience of life rather than being depressed by it, and accept our place in the universe. This is one of the most important steps towards spiritual growth in Zen and it's easy to see how the two philosophies complement each other.

Gain respect: Through meditation, no discrimination and working towards the selfless mind, *ikebana* helps us develop our best character.

Scents all the time: We can be always surrounded by the fragrance of flowers. Even when we feel a bit depressed, the scent of flowers always cheers us up. *Ikebana* artists know which flowers work best for him/her and his/her family and friends

Departing from any harmful thoughts: We may sometimes have evil or negative thoughts. When we face flowers, however, these thoughts disappear instantly. *Ikebana* can help keep our minds calm – a real bonus in today's world!

Peaceful mind: As we acquire peaceful mind through *ikebana*, we can nourish ourselves and live longer. In actual fact, statistics show that even today *ikebana* teachers are one of the occupation groups that live longest in Japan, a country with some of the oldest people in the world.

Graceful mind: Maintaining a peaceful mind from morning to evening, we can develop an understanding of the elegance of the natural world. We can nurture our gentleness and come closer to feeling at one with the universe – the experience of *satori* (enlightenment) in Zen. Many Japanese seem to find ultimate peace in realizing that they are a part of the nature. This also relates to Shinto philosophy.

Close to the Divine: We have more and more divine experiences in which we feel close to Buddha, or Gods or the Divine Spirit, depending on our own personal philosophy. Strengthening ties with the Divine was probably the most important value in the seventeenth century, and all of us could use more divine experiences in our lives – *ikebana* is one way to help us make contact with the elements of nature and the laws of the universe.

These ten virtues of *ikebana* remind us of this: if we have a chance to learn *ikebana*, it is important to be aware of the therapeutic and spiritual aspects that Japanese people have valued for centuries. If, however, we are learning only the basic patterns in design and skills to manipulate plants, we are not learning the essence of this wonderful art, the practice of which can lead us to make connections with our spiritual self in the same way Zen practitioners seek enlightenment through meditation. If we can find peace in our flower arrangements we can also find time to appreciate things in Nature that people often overlook because of their busy lives. It is also believed that we become more patient and tolerant of differences, not only in nature, but also in general. *Kadō* can inspire us to identify with beauty in all art forms. This is also a time when we feel close to Nature, which in turn provides relaxation for the mind, body, and soul.

Enlightenment is like
The reflection of the moon in water
The does not get wet
The water is not separated.

The Kensho Moment: Exercise

Scrying as a divination or meditational technique allows us to look into a reflective surface and see things in a different place and time. It is a method of seeing into parallel worlds, dimensions not our own, and realms normally forbidden from man. The use of a scrying bowl is very simple. The bowl should be wide and shallow, made of a non-reflective matte surface and should be dark in colour, with black being ideal. This can even be a permanent water-feature in our Zen garden and be dual-purpose.

The bowl should be kept clean and filled to the brim with water at all times and we begin by sitting comfortably within arm's reach of the bowl, and closing our eyes halfway. Begin by breathing in slowly through our nose, breathing inward until our lungs cannot fill any further. Then, we breathe out through our mouth, until we cannot possibly expel any more air from our lungs. This is called Full Breath. We repeat this for ten full breaths, and taking as much time as we need. During our breathing, we concentrate on becoming aware of the surface of the water – focusing our eyes on its surface to allow for attuning our eyes and mind to the shifting of perception that will occur during scrying. When we are ready, gaze into the surface of the water, focus on the surface, and slowly move a little to see it from a different angle; our mind will register any images that occur in a reflection of the trees and plants around us.

The full moon has long been considered a symbol of wisdom and intuition. Using the reflective surface of the garden bowl, we are relying on the moon to illuminate the water. Ensuring the bowl is full, we position our self so that we can see the moon's light reflected directly into the water. Stare into the water, looking for patterns, symbols or pictures depending on the phase of the moon reflected in the water. If we live near a natural body of water such as a garden pond or lake, we can perform water scrying with these larger 'bowls' instead.

Follow your own light
Be ordinary
Then you will see for yourself
That you are part of the whole.

Chapter Five

A Lesson from the Past for the Future

Ignore the brilliance of your intellect
and return to the unconscious vastness of unknowing.

All Japanese art forms, such as *chado* (the tea-ceremony), *ikebana* (flower arranging), *shodo* (calligraphy) and even martial arts are greatly influenced by the unique Zen philosophy, while the art forms themselves were transformed by Zen into a spiritual discipline focused on calmness, simplicity, and self-growth. In Japan, there is a tradition of studying art not only for art's sake but also for spiritual purposes and when this is practised with Zen principles in mind, art can be a peaceful journey and a way of self-cultivation – leading to calmness, serenity and concentration.

The teaching of Zen concerning the arts focuses on the importance of the mind-body-spirit unity, which is essential for the mastery of every art; while practising art with a Zen perception, the mind remains in the 'now' – being fully aware of the illusory nature of material life. In all honesty, it is probably correct to observe that without the influence of Zen, Japan would never have reached its high level of refinement and cultivation in the arts.

And yet the rustic charm of a valuable tea-bowl often appears unfinished to Western eyes; and the artist masterpieces such as Hasegawa Tohaku's *Pine Trees*; Tensho Shubun's *Reading in a Bamboo Grove* or Hiroshi Yoshida's *Fuji from Kawaguchi Lake* can leave the European viewer quite unmoved. Similarly, while the variety of musical scales used in traditional Japanese music can sound discordant, these scales have great significance within traditional culture. They provide a mystical and distinctive sound, which are given male and female characteristics, and represent the five basic elements of earth, water, fire, wood and metal. On more familiar ground the *shakuhachi* (bamboo flute) is often used to great effect in vintage film scores, while renowned Japanese classical and film-score composer Toru Takemitsu wrote many pieces for *shakuhachi* and orchestra, including his well-known *Celeste, Autumn* and *November Steps*.

Nevertheless, this appreciation of Japanese aesthetics has only recently caught the popular imagination in the West where it is viewed as an integral part of Zen philosophy; the concept of aesthetics in Japan is seen as an integral part of daily life. This set of ancient ideals that includes *wabi* (transient and stark beauty), *sabi* (the beauty of natural patina and ageing), and *yūgen* profound grace and subtlety), and these ideals, and others, underpin much of what is considered tasteful or beautiful.

And while Shinto is considered to be at the fountain-head of Japanese culture with its emphasis on the wholeness of nature and character in ethics, and its celebration of the landscape, the aesthetic ideals are most heavily influenced by Zen. In Buddhist tradition, all things are considered as either evolving from or dissolving into nothingness; this 'nothingness' is not empty space, it is rather a space of potentiality. If the seas represent potential then each thing is like a wave arising from it and returning to it; there are no permanent waves and at no point is a wave complete, even at its peak. Nature is seen as a dynamic whole that is to be admired and appreciated. This appreciation of nature has been fundamental to many Japanese aesthetic ideals, 'arts' and other cultural elements. In this respect, the notion of 'art' (or its conceptual equivalent) is also quite different from Western traditions. (*Zen Flesh, Zen Bones*)

Wabi and *sabi* refers to a mindful approach to everyday life. Over time their meanings overlapped and converged until they are unified into *Wabi-sabi*, the aesthetic defined as the beauty of things 'imperfect, impermanent, and incomplete'. Things in bud, or things in decay, for example, are more evocative of *wabi-sabi* than things in full bloom because they suggest the transience of things. As things come and go, they reveal signs of their coming or going, and these signs are considered to be beautiful; in this, beauty is an altered state of consciousness that can be seen in the mundane and simple. The signatures of nature can be so subtle that it takes a quiet mind and a cultivated eye to discern them. In Zen philosophy there are seven aesthetic principles for achieving *wabi-sabi* that we can easily learn to incorporate into our Western pagan idealism:

- *Fukinsei*: asymmetry, irregularity;
- *Kanso*: simplicity;
- *Koko*: basic, weathered;
- *Shizen*: without pretence, natural;
- *Yugen*: subtly profound grace, not obvious;
- *Datsuzoku*: unbounded by convention, free;
- *Seijaku*: tranquillity.

Each of these things is found in nature but can also suggest virtues of human character and appropriateness of behaviour. This, in turn suggests that virtue and civility can be instilled through an appreciation of, and practice in, the arts just as aesthetic ideals have an ethical connotation and pervades much of Japanese culture. Or, as Sei Shonagon writes:

On the third day of the Third Month [March] I like to see the sun shining bright and calm in the spring sky. Now is the time when the peach trees come into bloom, and what a sight it is! The willows too are most charming at this season, with the buds still enclosed like silk worms in their cocoons. After the leaves have spread out,

I find them unattractive; in fact all trees lose their charm once the blossoms have begun to scatter. It is a great pleasure to break off a long, beautifully flowering branch from a cherry tree and to arrange it in a large vase. What a delightful task to perform when a visitor is seated nearby conversing! ... I am even happier if a butterfly or a small bird flutters prettily near the flowers and I can see its face.

The Kensho Moment: Exercise

Wa is a Japanese cultural concept usually translated into English as 'harmony'. It implies a peaceful unity and conformity within a social group, in which members prefer the continuation of a harmonious community over their personal interests. In Japanese society acting untrue to one's inner beliefs is not only accepted but is its own moral virtue. The most important of all Japanese social values is *wa*, and if achieving *wa* requires a bit of play-acting, then so be it.

The Japanese distinguish between *honne* – an individual's true feelings – and *tatemai* – the face one wears in public. When our *honne* is at odds with the harmony of the group, a mature, virtuous person is expected to rise above his or her own selfish feelings and, for the welfare of the majority, put on a good face. To 'stick up for what you stand for' is not a Japanese ideal. Most Japanese understand there's a difference between this public play-acting and reality, but nearly everyone is agreed upon its importance. In other words, what those in the West may perceive as hypocritical, dishonest behaviour is not only tolerated in Japan, but esteemed as good citizenship. This is, of course, no different to the traditional Old Craft saying that a witch has three faces – one we show to the world, one we keep for our friends and family, and one we show only to our gods.

There is, of course, also an inner harmony – or sense of spiritual peace and tranquillity that can be achieved by moving from Concentration to Meditation, from Meditation to Contemplation – 'an utterly impersonal awareness of the essence

71

of the thing observed'. Aesthetically, *wa* is fundamental to all harmonious living, yet it goes beyond aesthetics. *Wa* also refers to a 'gentleness of spirit', so harmony also refers to an internal feeling or approach to art and to life. No doubt the particulars will change depending on the case and circumstances, but the concept is the same: in all things harmony – and since harmony exists inherently in the cosmos and on our planet, we can benefit ourselves and others by learning from lessons found in Nature. *Wa* has direct applications for our personal lives, our relationships, and our whole approach to life and work ... and should our personal *wa* be knocked out of kilter, life immediately becomes unbalanced and restive until our inner harmony is restored by implementing:

Concentration: First, we learn to develop the power of concentration which is the fundamental discipline of Zen. The conscious mind has been described as being like a grasshopper ... as soon as we attempt to concentrate on something in silence our mind hops about hither and thither. This happens to everybody who tries it at first and we can get over it. Concentration is the result of directed thought; an ability to give our attention or thought to a single object or activity. If we develop great powers of concentration, it means we're able to focus all our attention on the matter at hand. Whatever and whenever our thoughts are directed down a certain channel without being deflected – that attitude is then termed as concentration.

- If trying to restore our state of intellectual or emotional balance, it helps to concentrate on something that gives us a feeling of peace or extreme pleasure – to the extent that it excludes everything else from our thoughts.
- Deep breathing exercises also give an enhanced ability to concentrate. In fact, the first thing we notice when we do deep breathing exercises is the mental reaction we get. We

notice it far quicker than any physical reaction; the mental reaction is almost immediate. The physical reaction – better health, glowing skin, enhanced magnetism – comes later.

Meditation: This can be defined as a practice where an individual focuses their mind on a particular object, thought or activity to achieve a mentally clear and emotionally calm state. Meditation can also help us to understand our own mind. We can learn how to transform our mind from negative to positive, from disturbed to peaceful, from unhappy to happy. In fact, overcoming a negative mindset and cultivating constructive thoughts is the purpose of the transforming meditations found in the Buddhist tradition. This is a profound spiritual practice we can enjoy throughout the day, not just while seated in meditation.

- The first stage of meditation is to block out all distractions and make our mind clearer and more lucid. This can be accomplished by practising a simple breathing meditation. Choose a quiet place and sit in a comfortable position; if we wish, we can sit in a chair. The most important thing is to keep our back straight to prevent our mind from becoming sluggish or sleepy.
- We sit with our eyes partially closed and turn our attention to our breathing. We breathe naturally, preferably through the nostrils, without attempting to control our breath, and we try to become aware of the sensation of the breath as it enters and leaves the nostrils. This sensation is our object of meditation. We should try to concentrate on it to the exclusion of everything else.
- At first, our mind will be very busy, and we might even feel that the meditation is making our mind busier; but in reality we are just becoming more aware of how busy our mind actually is. There will be a great temptation to follow

the different thoughts as they arise, but we should resist this and remain focused single-pointedly on the sensation of the breath. If we discover that our mind has wandered and is following our thoughts, we should immediately return it to the breath. We should repeat this as many times as necessary until the mind settles on the breath ... and we start to relax.

Contemplation is something slightly different. It is a state of mind where the thought is controlled; but the mind is left open to receive. If we were to concentrate on a Japanese *koi* we would examine the fish very thoroughly, even count the fins, scales and so on: if we were to contemplate on the same fish we would leave our mind open to learn something about its environment, its physical function, its mental function and so on. Similarly, we might choose to concentrate and contemplate on an artistic drawing – one of Sesshū Tōyō's splashed ink landscapes, *Haboku-Sansui* for instance. First of all, we concentrate on that particular picture where the painter avoids strongly defined outlines, with shapes indicated by colour washes in lighter and darker tones. We notice the work slowly revealing itself to us, emerging from the undefined forms is the suggestion of misty mountains in the background. In the foreground are cliffs and bushes, and the triangular roofline and sloping banner for a wine shop with vertical lines forming a fence. Below is indicated the flat surface of a body of water, with two people to the right in a rowing boat ... In the next stage, contemplation, we would go much deeper and look not only into that picture, but deep into the heart and mind of the artist who had painted that picture, using the picture as our focal point.

- During contemplation, if we are doing breathing exercises for instance, would make us aware of exactly what is happening to us. Not only would we concentrate on guiding the breath and *prana*, but we would learn what is taking place within us as we do it. It is a much deeper state than concentration.

- Contemplation is that state of consciousness which brings us clairvoyant power. It must, because the basis of contemplation is a clairvoyant perception, a kind of spiritual intuition. We would not only know about that picture, but we would know about the person who painted it. If we contemplated a bit further, we would not only know about the person who painted it but we would know about the canvas it was painted on, the brushes it was painted with, and even the atomic structure of the pigments of the paint that was used. That is taking contemplation as far as you can take contemplation.

Perhaps at this stage we should return to the comments made by Dr James Fox following his visit to Ryoan-ji Zen garden at the Temple of the Dragon at Peace. He found that when contemplating the garden and as time passed something remarkable happened: the gaps between the stones came alive and the emptiness filled up with a vast panorama of the world – then, just like that, it was nothing more than a group of rocks once again. 'If this garden has a meaning it is something that ultimately comes from within ourselves – this garden is a blank canvas that allows the mind to wander,' he mused, still in a contemplatory frame of mind.

Then we begin to understand how the sky, the flowers, the trees and the beautiful landscape speak to the Shintoist and Zen practitioner of beauty and purity. And so now we can look upon such sights with reverence because we also feel the awe in the presence of that pure loveliness of which we are so deeply aware … and the sacred essence that manifests in all those multiple forms. We realise *kami* and people exist within the same world and share its interrelated complexity and that *kami* refers particularly to that power of phenomena which inspires this sense of wonder and awe [the sacred] in the beholder, testifying to its divinity. Nature is venerated and nothing is too small to be of importance.

Those who cannot feel the littleness
of great things in themselves, are apt to overlook
the greatness of little things in others.
Kakuzo Okakura

Footnote: From me flows what you call time …

'At a time when the light of civilisation flickered dimly in the rest of the world, the Japanese, remote in their distant islands, were developing a lifestyle quite unrelated to the experience in the West,' wrote Robin Duke in his Introduction to *The Pillow Book of Sei Shonagon*. The development of the traditional arts of the time was more than of superficial importance in a society 'wholly preoccupied with art and letters, quick to criticise a poor stroke of the brush or a faulty line of verse'. Art played the central role in society. First and foremost as a social essential came poetry and failure to compose an instant poem to suit an occasion, to recognise an allusion or complete a quotation was a disaster.

If, however, we wish to make a serious study of Zen within its Buddhist context then it requires more than reading a few books, learning to meditate, and hi-jacking a few practical exercises. In contrast to the monotheistic religions, however, there are no absolutes in Shinto or Zen There is no absolute right and wrong, and nobody is perfect. Shinto is an optimistic faith, as humans are thought to be fundamentally good, and evil is believed to be caused by evil spirits. Consequently, the purpose of most Shinto rituals is to keep away evil spirits by purification, prayers and offerings to the *kami*. While one of the basic precepts of Zen is to live life in the moment, to be truly alive and aware right now, without diverting ourselves with thoughts of either the past or the future. Following this path, it is ultimately possible to realise your true potential, releasing creative energy we never knew we had.

Or as Sei Shonogon recorded in her *Pillow Book* all those centuries ago:

It was a clear, moonlit night a little after the tenth of the Eight Month, Her Majesty, who was residing in the Empress's Office, sat by the edge of the veranda while Ukon no Naishi played the flute for her. The other ladies in attendance sat together, talking and laughing; but I stayed by myself, leaning against one of the pillars between the main hall and the veranda.

'Why so silent?' said Her Majesty. 'Say something. It is sad when you do not speak.'

'I am gazing at the autumn moon,' I replied.

'Ah yes,' she remarked, 'that is just what you should have said.'

Nevertheless, as Paul Reps observes in *Zen Flesh, Zen Bones*, 'Old Zen was so fresh it became treasured and remembered. Here are fragments of its skin, flesh, bones, but not its marrow – never found in words. The enlightenment for which Zen aims, for which Zen exists, comes of itself – as consciousness. One moment it does not exist, the next it does.' Such heightened moments of enlightenment cannot be reduced to mere words and like the old soldier trying to explain military black humour – 'I guess you had to have been there.'

The contemplative aspect of Zen meditation, however, *is* to show that one mind can never understand everything and enables the mind to wander in any direction it pleases. It pursues the unanswerable, the mysterious, because the answer isn't the point of meditation – it is the searching for understanding while appreciating that it is a search that will never end – and explains why we should value the unknowable.

All that is left is silence and a finger pointing the way.

In truth, we can embrace the philosophy of Zen whatever our religious persuasion. There is no reason why we can't use symbols of our own faith as a point of focus in the home or garden. Zen regards the whole world as sacred and in a certain sense Zen is feeling life instead of feeling something about life.

And while Shinto has always represented the lure of the outdoor spaces – the sand, the wind, the stars, the waves, the hum of the insects, the music of the waterfall, the animist in us all believes that the same wonderful forces that move in Nature move in ourselves. There is no difference because there is no dividing line between divine and human because our belief and our lifestyle have entered into each other to such an extent that it is almost impossible to tell where one begins and the other ends. To the thoughtful among us this is as it should be. Why should belief be something 'added onto' a person's life?

Just as Jon Moore intended in *Zen Druid*, Western Animism also attempts to strip animistic thought down to its basic principles and structures, and to also offer a celebration of earth-based spirituality in a form that requires no embellishment. Here we remove the customary intellectual dismissal of animism belonging to primitive culture and elevate it to the sophisticated heights of an uncomplicated connection with the divine.

It is not the results of our actions
That we are working for, but the
Fulfilment of just doing.

Sources & Bibliography

Eastern Religions [Shinto], C Scott Littleton (dbponline)

The Floral Calendar of Japan, T D Makino (Tourist Library of Japan)

Historical Dictionary of Shinto, Stuart Picken (NLA)

Infinite Spaces, Ed Joe Earl (Galileo)

A Japanese Touch for Your Garden, Kiyoshi Seike (Kodansha)

Living by Zen, D T Suzuki (Rider)

The Pillow Book of Sei Shonagon, trans Ivan Morris (Folio)

Sakuteiki, trans Jiro Takei and Marc P Keane (Tuttle)

Shinto, the Kami Way, Sokyo Ono (Tuttle)

Shinto, a Short History, Inoue Nobutaka (Routledge)

The Three Pillars of Zen, Philip Kapleau (Beacon)

The True Face of Japan, Komakichi Nohara (Jarrold 1936)

The World's Great Religions, Floyd H Ross and Tynette Hills (Crest)

Zen Druid: A Paganism for the 21st Century, Jon Moore (Learbooks)

Zen Flesh, Zen Bones, Paul Reps & Nyogen Senzaki (Pelican)

Zen Mind, Beginner's Mind, Shunryu Suzuki (Weatherhill)

Zen Training, Katsuki Sekida (Weatherhill)

Zen, A Way of Life, Christmas Humphreys (Hodder & Stoughton)

MOON
BOOKS

PAGANISM & SHAMANISM

What is Paganism? A religion, a spirituality, an alternative belief system, nature worship? You can find support for all these definitions (and many more) in dictionaries, encyclopaedias, and text books of religion, but subscribe to any one and the truth will evade you. Above all Paganism is a creative pursuit, an encounter with reality, an exploration of meaning and an expression of the soul. Druids, Heathens, Wiccans and others, all contribute their insights and literary riches to the Pagan tradition. Moon Books invites you to begin or to deepen your own encounter, right here, right now.

If you have enjoyed this book, why not tell other readers by posting a review on your preferred book site.

Medicine for the Soul
The Complete Book of Shamanic Healing
Ross Heaven
All you will ever need to know about shamanic healing and how to
become your own shaman...
Paperback: 978-1-78099-419-2 ebook: 978-1-78099-420-8

Shaman Pathways – The Druid Shaman
Exploring the Celtic Otherworld
Danu Forest
A practical guide to Celtic shamanism with exercises and
techniques as well as traditional lore for exploring the Celtic
Otherworld.
Paperback: 978-1-78099-615-8 ebook: 978-1-78099-616-5

Traditional Witchcraft for the Woods and Forests
A Witch's Guide to the Woodland with Guided Meditations and
Pathworking
Mélusine Draco
A Witch's guide to walking alone in the woods, with guided
meditations and pathworking.
Paperback: 978-1-84694-803-9 ebook: 978-1-84694-804-6

Wild Earth, Wild Soul
A Manual for an Ecstatic Culture
Bill Pfeiffer
Imagine a nature-based culture so alive and so connected,
spreading like wildfire. This book is the first flame...
Paperback: 978-1-78099-187-0 ebook: 978-1-78099-188-7

Naming the Goddess
Trevor Greenfield
Naming the Goddess is written by over eighty adherents and
scholars of Goddess and Goddess Spirituality.
Paperback: 978-1-78279-476-9 ebook: 978-1-78279-475-2

Shapeshifting into Higher Consciousness
Heal and Transform Yourself and Our World with Ancient
Shamanic and Modern Methods
Llyn Roberts
Ancient and modern methods that you can use every day to
transform yourself and make a positive difference in the world.
Paperback: 978-1-84694-843-5 ebook: 978-1-84694-844-2

Readers of ebooks can buy or view any of these bestsellers by
clicking on the live link in the title. Most titles are published in
paperback and as an ebook. Paperbacks are available in traditional
bookshops. Both print and ebook formats are available online.

Find more titles and sign up to our readers' newsletter at
http://www.johnhuntpublishing.com/paganism
Follow us on Facebook at https://www.facebook.com/MoonBooks
and Twitter at https://twitter.com/MoonBooksJHP